INVENTIONS EVERY *MAN'S MAN* SHOULD KNOW ABOUT

MANVENTIONS

FROM CRUISE CONTROL TO CORDLESS DRILLS— INVENTIONS *Men Can't Live Without*

INSIDE YOU WILL FIND:

1. *PONG, CLAY POKER CHIPS, WII*
2. *GOLF CARTS, CLEATS, SHIN GUARDS*
3. *MICROWAVES, POP-TOP BEER CANS, HOT SAUCE*
4. *URINALS, DRIVE-THROUGH RESTAURANTS, ROLLER COASTERS, ATM MACHINES*
5. *HDTV, DVR, INSTANT REPLAY*
6. *IPODS, SUPERHEROES, ELECTRIC GUITARS*
7. *SUPERGLUE, CORDLESS TOOLS, RIDING LAWN MOWERS*
8. *ED MEDS, BIKINIS, LINGERIE*
9. *CRUISE CONTROL, GPS*

TESTOSTERONE-DRIVEN >>> FUEL-GUZZLING INVENTIONS

AMUSING MAN-TASTIC FACTS, MAN-DATES, AND MORE!

BOBBY MERCER
author of *How Do You Light a Fart?*

Published by
Adams Media, a division of F+W Media, Inc.
57 Littlefield Street, Avon, MA 02322. U.S.A.
www.adamsmedia.com

ISBN 10: 1-4405-1073-3
ISBN 13: 978-1-4405-1073-1
eISBN 10: 1-4405-1074-1
eISBN 13: 978-1-4405-1074-8

Printed in the United States of America.

10 9 8 7 6 5 4 3 2 1

Library of Congress Cataloging-in-Publication Data
is available from the publisher.

This publication is designed to provide accurate and authoritative information with regard to the subject matter covered. It is sold with the understanding that the publisher is not engaged in rendering legal, accounting, or other professional advice. If legal advice or other expert assistance is required, the services of a competent professional person should be sought.

—From a *Declaration of Principles* jointly adopted by a Committee of the American Bar Association and a Committee of Publishers and Associations

Many of the designations used by manufacturers and sellers to distinguish their product are claimed as trademarks. Where those designations appear in this book and Adams Media was aware of a trademark claim, the designations have been printed with initial capital letters.

This book is available at quantity discounts for bulk purchases.
For information, please call 1-800-289-0963.

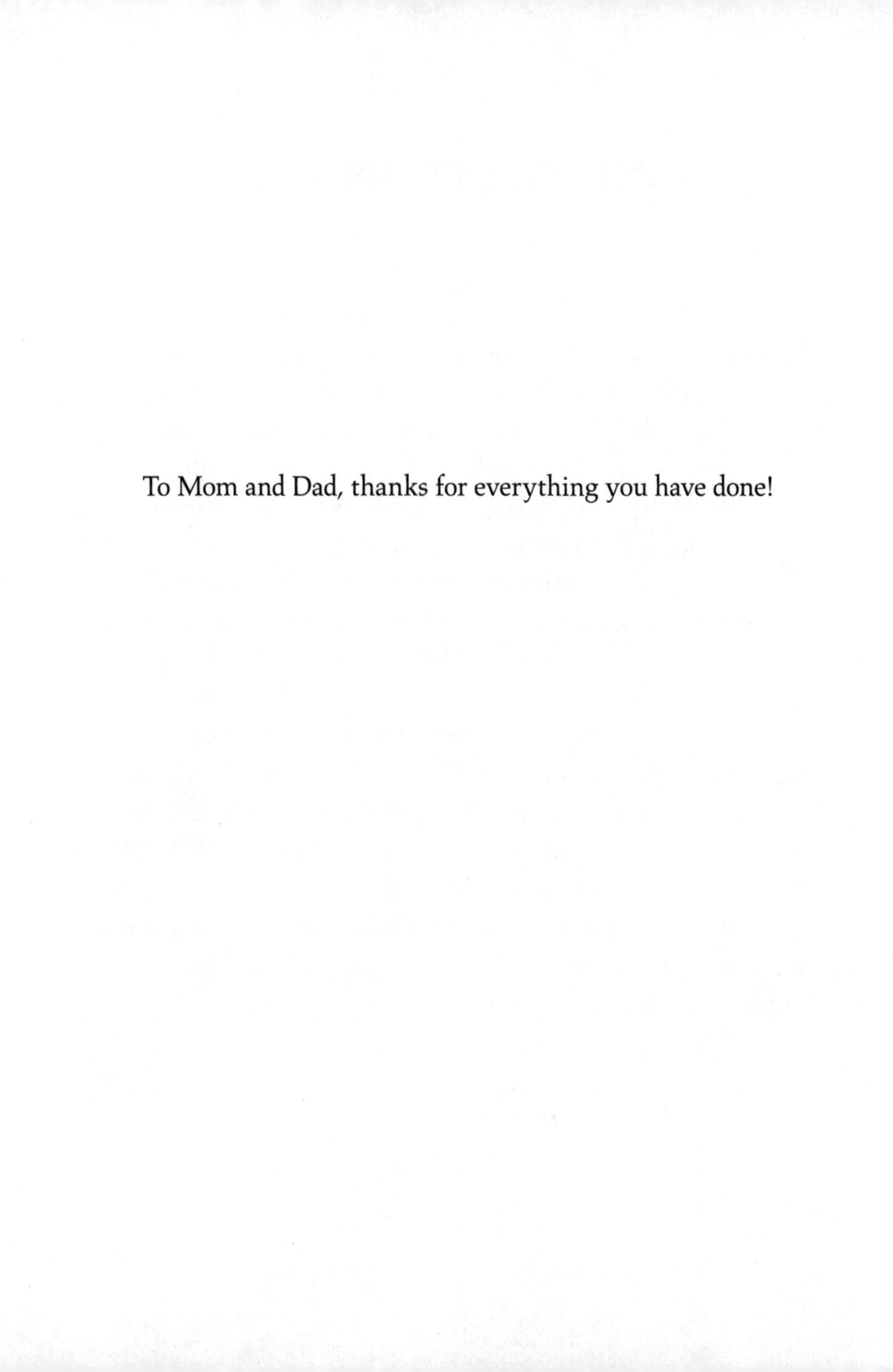

To Mom and Dad, thanks for everything you have done!

ACKNOWLEDGMENTS

Books don't happen without tons of people. I'd like to thank all the people who helped this idea become reality. Kathy Green for believing in the idea and for being the best agent in the business. Andrea Norville, Katie Corcoran Lytle, and the talented, creative people at Adams for helping shepherd this book through.

I'd like to thank my parents and in-laws for all of their help: Buzz and Joyce Mercer, Richard and Nancy Canamucio. And all of my great man friends who lent their ideas and encouragement; this list includes the following (and probably a few I will overlook): Jeff Andrews, David Burdette, Rich Canamucio, Matt Daigle, Mike Flowe, Robert Frost, Mike Garity, Jeff Gibson, Aaron Greene, John Hemmer, Bill Huddleston, Matt Kissling, Mitch Leonard, Scott Lowery, Rob Lucas, Pat McCool, Josh McEntire, Joe Potter, David Powell, Greg Robinson, Marvin Smith, Bobby Somerville, Jamie Thompson, Bill Van Cleve, Rex Wells, Danny Wilkins, and Sergey Zalevskiy.

Most of all, I'd like to thank my personal superhero, my wife, Michele. And a special thanks to our two sidekicks: Nicole and Jordan.

CONTENTS

INTRODUCTION

It's often said that necessity is the mother of invention. People see a need and start tinkering and practical inventions like the cotton gin and long underwear are born. These inventions make life easier, which is nice, but I'm a man, so I tend to be more enthralled by manventions. What are manventions? Amazing hair-curling, bicep-building, adrenaline-pumping inventions for men by people who know what men want.

Little boys love their toys, but kids grow out of stuff like that, right? Well, not if those toys are replaced with adult iterations that are bigger, better, faster, louder, and even more extreme. Staring at your older sister's best friend in a bikini is nice but forty-two hot scantily clad women on the pages of the *SI* swimsuit issue are better. Hand saws are functional, but a compound miter saw packs more power. You can mow your yard with an environmentally friendly push mower, but a 42-inch, zero-turn riding lawn mower is more manly. Cheap vodka will get you drunk, but twelve-year-old, cask-aged scotch makes getting there more enjoyable. The old adage "the only difference between men and boys is the price of their toys" is correct. And there's nothing like an over-the-top manvention to make us glad to be men.

So, cozy up in your La-Z-Boy, crack a cold Coors Light, and read on, or perhaps sit majestically on the throne and do your business. Either way, here they are—the best manventions on the planet.

CHAPTER 1

Books, Movies, and Music:

Special Effects, Stratocasters, Superheroes, and Beyond

INSIDE YOU WILL FIND:

- ☑ *The* Star Wars *Trilogy*
- ☑ *The Fender Stratocaster*
- ☑ *Dick Flicks*
- ☑ *Spider-Man, HellBoy, and Stan Lee*
- ☑ **Pokémon** *and* **Watchmen**
- ☑ *Superman, Batman, and More*

Men like loud. We love music that makes your ears bleed. We love movie explosions that inspire us to install twelve-foot-high speakers and subwoofers in our living rooms. We love gun battles, car chases, and half-naked women (sometimes they can be loud too—if we're lucky). Fortunately, we live in an age where you can leave a concert and not be able to hear for a week and a half afterwards, where movie mayhem runs rampant, and even our books highlight explosions. So pop in your earplugs as we explore the wonderful world of manly music and movies.

THE *STAR WARS* TRILOGY

The first *Star Wars* film exploded on theater screens in 1977. A relatively low-budget sci-fi action flick, it was a megahit even though the studio execs weren't sure it was going to pay off. Little did they realize that going to the movies would be forever changed: Men could now take a date to see a flick with exploding starships. No wonder we left the theaters cheering.

Lucas was (and still is) a wizard with special effects and surround sound—two of *man*kind's great loves. Sitting in the dark as the opening scene enveloped us with sound added a new level to our enjoyment. The rumbling started behind us and pretty soon we were sitting right under a star destroyer fighting its way through space. Pretty. Freakin'. Amazing. After that we were treated to light sabers, blasters, and the deep breathing that made the movie a smash. Lucas continued to push the boundaries in computer-aided graphics and sound and added more man-friendly special effects in subsequent movies. And if that wasn't good enough, he also added a little star power, some half-naked women, and the

> ### MAN-TASTIC FACT
>
> David Prowse, the British actor who donned the Darth Vader costume in the original *Star Wars* trilogy, also played Frankenstein's monster in at least three movies.

> ### MAN-TASTIC FACT
>
> Al Pacino was considered for the role of Han Solo.

MAN-DATE

When the original *Star Wars* movie was released in 1977, there was almost no advance publicity since the studio wasn't sure a sci-fi movie would work.

best movie villain ever to grace the silver screen.

Let's be honest here, no guy alive will ever forget Princess Leia's slave costume; it's an image that is forever seared into minds of men everywhere. Han Solo also gave our dates something to lust over, and many of us made out very well as a result of that lust. But, despite the half-naked hotties running around with light sabers, the star of the *Star Wars* movies was none other than Darth Vader: the greatest villain of all time. Darth was menacing, mean, and wicked and put the *Star Wars* trilogy light years away from anything else that was—or is—on the market.

Star Wars changed movies for men forever. With sci-fi movie mayhem, great villains, and hot women, date nights would never be the same. *Star Wars* may have made Lucas a gazillionaire, but it also made us proud to be men. George Lucas, may the Force be with you.

MAN-TASTIC FACT

Blaster fire in the first *Star Wars* was actually created by a hammer hitting tightly strung antenna wire.

THE FENDER STRATOCASTER

Men love music, and we like it loud. And hands down, the guitar is one of our favorite musical instruments. (Let's be honest, at one point or another we've all air-guitared along with one of the legends of rock.)

So how did we make the fabulous guitar a louder instrument? We added steel instead of nylon strings and the guitar became louder, but that wasn't enough to lift it to front-stage status. It took electricity to pump up the volume, and in the 1920s, advances in electronic amplification came to the rescue. Lloyd Loar, an engineer working for the Gibson guitar company, developed the magnetic pickup, which was placed beneath the steel string and created a magnetic field. The vibrating string disturbed the magnetic field and the disturbances were converted to electric current and amplified electronically. Finally, we got

MAN-TASTIC FACT

The world's largest Fender Stratocaster welcomes riders to the Rock 'n' Roller Coaster Starring Aerosmith at Disney World in Orlando, Florida.

the power of volume control and garage bands everywhere rejoiced!

Jazz and country musicians first embraced the concept of the electric guitar, but it would take some innovative rebels like Les Paul to make it more mainstream. Paul had experimented with microphones on acoustic guitars for years, but the magnetic pickup was what he had been waiting for. Now, mankind had volume control and rock gods could also electronically alter their music. Paul was also one of the first to create a solid-body electric guitar without a hollow air chamber, which allowed guitars to be smaller—and easier to whirl around on stage. His electric guitar was called "The Log" because it was made from common 4×4 lumber. Can you imagine a trip to Home Depot to get lumber to make a guitar? How sweet is that?

> ***MAN-TASTIC FACT***
>
> 1970s music legend Steve Miller ("Fly Like an Eagle," "Abracadabra," and "Take the Money and Run") is the godson of guitar legend Les Paul. In fact, Paul is reported to have taught the five-year-old Miller his first chords. Steve, in turn, passed on his music acumen to others by teaching his Texas classmate Boz Scaggs ("Lido Shuffle" and "Lowdown") a few chords so they could play in a band together.

The Fender Stratocaster, a.k.a. the Strat, is the king of electric guitars and is one of the greatest musical manventions ever invented. A piece of art miles away from "The Log," the Strat has been played by almost every guitar god of the last fifty years, from Buddy Holly to Jimi Hendrix to Eric Clapton. Dudes love these guys, but the music the Strat created has also helped us get laid for years. Need I remind you of the 1980s? Six cans of hairspray, a little eyeliner, and a couple of electric guitars were all it took to get women swooning. And where there are swooning women, you will find guys. Thank you Fender Stratocaster, from the bottom of our rock-loving hearts.

> **MAN-TASTIC FACT**
>
> The singer Meat Loaf was a vegetarian for over fifteen years. Ironic, right?

DICK FLICKS

Chicks have chick flicks, those sappy, mindless movies that always star Julia Roberts, Katherine Heigl, or Matthew McConaughey, and men have dick flicks, action-packed movies with lots of gratuitous violence, cool cars, neat special effects, and hot girls. Men go to chick flicks to get laid. We go to dick flicks to get an adrenaline rush, and the fact that the hot girl will usually get naked is a bonus. All of these kick-ass qualities give dick flicks their honored spot on the manvention list.

You can't have a great dick flick without a really cool lead star. Tough-guy John Wayne was the dude that every guy wanted to be in the early days of talkies, and in

> **MAN-TASTIC FACT**
>
> Nine hexagonal pencils can be made from the same amount of wood as eight round pencils.

MAN-DATE

Although dick flicks hardly ever win an Oscar, the name *Oscar* has a curious origin. The awards started in 1929, but the Academy Award's nickname came from Margaret Herrick, executive secretary of the Academy, in 1931. When she first saw the little statue, she remarked how it looked just like her Uncle Oscar. The slang name wasn't officially adopted until 1939.

the '70s and '80s the heroes became muscle heads like Schwarzenegger and Stallone. Bruce Willis entered the realm just because of his ability to be a smart-ass, and some of the coolest lead stars were from the horror genre like Freddy, Michael Myers, and Leatherface.

In addition to a rough and tumble hero, dick flicks also need a stunning beauty for that hero to fall in love with. And if the hero is too stupid to fall in love with her—or if the "hero" is a horror lead—we guys need eye candy. After all, a hot girl makes it easier to part with something like $33 for a ticket and the small popcorn combo.

All dick flicks need really cool special effects and gadgets, and the movies give these to us in spades. From Jedis fighting

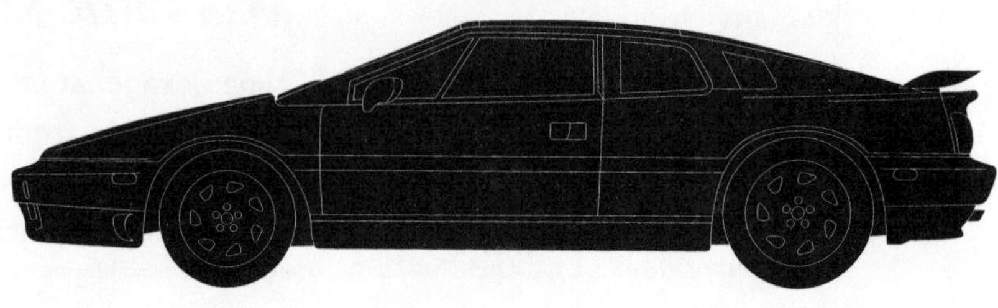

with light sabers to ordinary cars that morph into world-killing machines, computers have given us the special effects that make any dick flick amazing. Gone are the cheesy effects that populated Hollywood twenty years ago. Stunt people were amazing with what they could do, but they aren't nearly as good as a nerd with a computer. As far as gadgets are concerned, we've seen cars like Bullitt's Mustang, guns like Dirty Harry's Magnum, or even weapons like Wolverine's adamantium claws. But no one has better gadgets than our favorite spy, James Bond. The James Bond franchise is the epitome of dick flicks. 007 always has a cool car, hot babe, and tons of action. We don't care if the stunts are hardly believable, we'll still plunk down the money for the ticket and go. Why? Gadgets and stunts aside, we all want to get a good look at the latest Bond girl. Trust me when I tell you that all the guys watching a James Bond movie are just sitting in the seats imagining ordering a vodka martini (shaken, not stirred) and then bedding the girl.

MAN-TASTIC FACT

The creator of the 007 books was Ian Fleming. Ian also wrote a children's book, *Chitty Chitty Bang Bang: The Magical Car*, that was turned into a film.

Many dick flicks have morphed into franchises that continue to show up every two years, which is awesome. There's nothing wrong with a new story—or complete remake—every few years. A few franchises have seen numerous stars in the lead role. In fact, Batman has been played by virtually every male in Hollywood. And some franchises (like *Rocky*) would have been better if they had replaced their leading man occasionally; Stallone fighting at sixty-plus was hard to watch.

So to sum up, a cool lead actor + cool gadgets + violent special effects + a hot girl = a pretty amazing dick flick that almost any guy will pony up the cash to see.

SPIDER-MAN, HELLBOY, AND STAN LEE

Men have been telling stories with art ever since we could hold a pencil. Using art to tell stories started with fur-wearing cavemen who created their man-art by slapping a little paint on the wall. Next thing you know, pictures of buffalo hunts were forever written on the wall of the cave. Bet their parents weren't thrilled. Today, cute little flowers and triangular houses start out as the object of our art obsession, but we grow more twisted as we get older. What man hasn't drawn a giant penis on a school desk sometime during his life? Or how about a naked drawing of the hot teacher when we were in junior high? All this art talk makes me wonder if my dicktograph is still inscribed on hot Ms. Brumbeloe's desk?

Man's love of art inspired one of our favorite manventions: the comic book. After all, what's wrong with a book with pictures? Millions of pimple-faced, squeaky-voiced young men grew up reading their favorite comic books. Cute and world-saving when we were young, comic books grew as we did, and

MAN-DATE

National Comics #18 featured Uncle Sam helping fight off an attack on Pearl Harbor. The comic was released in November 1941—one month before Pearl Harbor was actually bombed—and featured the Germans bombing Battleship Row (not the Japanese, for those of you who slept through U.S. history).

the characters took on a more sinister bent as we aged. The comic-book movies of today are consumer-pleasing, sterile versions of the books we love. The actual comic books of today are darker and more twisted than the "boyventions" of our youth.

Horror, war, and detective stories have all been featured in comic books, and characters like Sgt. Rock, Spawn, Hellboy, and the Crypt-Keeper are just a few of the comic men who helped us through our puberty-driven youth. And we can thank one Stanley Lieber (better known as Stan Lee) for helping comics grow up with us and for taking them to the dark place where they live today. Lee pushed his editor into publishing comic books written and drawn for a more mature audience, and his creations (Spider-Man, the Hulk, and the X-Men) moved comic books into more serious topics that men embraced. The comic-book-created superheroes morphed from kid-friendly to weird and almost twisted male fantasies. They allow us to be men . . . without giving up the things we loved when we were boys. And the endless amounts of toys, movies, and graphic novels just serve to make a good thing even better.

POKÉMON AND WATCHMEN

300, The Sandman, Watchmen, and *V for Vendetta* are just a few of the famous graphic novels that have kept us entertained for years. And, as you can see from that list, they are also the source of countless movies. Graphic novels are just comic books on steroids. They are longer than comic books and are usually distributed by traditional book publishers directly to bookstores, not just newsstands. Graphic novels have actually been around longer than comic books, and many of the early graphic novels were just collections of daily comic strips, just as some graphic novels today are a collection of individual comic books, like Frank Miller's *Batman: Dark Knight* series.

Graphic novels have grown in popularity in the last twenty years. The old adage that a picture is worth a thousand words perfectly describes the graphic novel today as Hollywood has mined graphic novels for story and movie ideas, looking for the next blockbuster moneymaker. But this graphic-novel-to-movie phenomenon is not as new as you might think. In fact, *The Mask, Time Cop,* and *Road to Perdition* are three graphic novels that successfully came to life on the silver screen years ago. And recent additions to the graphic-novel-turned-movie list include *Sin City, 300,* and *From Hell.* All of these guy favorites go way beyond the superhero comic-book movies and hold a special place in our hearts.

Another form of graphic novel, *manga* (Japanese for comics), has developed a cult following around the world. In fact, most anime (Japanese animation) starts out as manga that is then copied for shows and films. Pokémon is the world's best-known manga and anime story. You see, Americans aren't the only ones to rip off other art forms to make money.

Graphic novels are decidedly more adult than standard comic books, which men are more than okay with. I'm not going to lie, we sometimes crave gratuitous sex and violence, and graphic novels more than fill the bill for testosterone-driven men everywhere.

MAN-TASTIC FACT

Pokémon comes from a romanized Japanese abbreviation for Pocket Monsters. And while we are on the subject, shouldn't abbreviation be a shorter word?

SUPERMAN, BATMAN, AND MORE

The ability to do superhuman feats and look cool at the same time makes superheroes a definite man favorite. And that doesn't even take their gadgets, powers, secret lairs, sexual innuendos, and secret identities into account. Superheroes satisfy a longing inside males to be physically stronger, have cool powers, and be envied. What could possibly be better?

Superman was the first superhero. Hell, the name *superhero* even came from mild-mannered Clark Kent's crime-fighting alter ego. The creators, Jerry Siegel and Joe Shuster, pitched the idea for Superman to numerous publishers. After five years of rejections, Detective Comics (later DC Comics) finally introduced the man of steel to the world in 1938. Unfortunately, Siegel and Shuster got screwed on the deal. Detective Comics paid them a princely sum of $130 for thirteen pages and the rights to the character. What the hell were Siegel and Shuster thinking? They continued to work for DC comics until 1946 and made good money, but they were only paid a fraction of what DC made off the rights to Superman. After DC spun off Superboy, the pair got fed up and sued the comic-book company. They spent all of their money on legal fees, and they also got fired. Broke, they agreed to an out-of-court settlement with DC for just $200,000. They got royalties from Superboy but had to permanently give up the rights to Superman. Siegel and Shuster struggled financially until their deaths. If only a superhero could have read their initial contract. What about Lawyer Man?

MAN-TASTIC FACT

In the original comic-book story, a radioactive spider bites Peter Parker (Spider-Man) and gives him his superpowers. Parker then built and learned how to use the cool web-slinging contraption as part of his costume. In the recent movie series, a genetically engineered spider bites Parker and the web slingers actually grow in his arms.

The next great superhero was a perfect manvention: an ordinary guy with tons of money and really cool gadgets. After all, men love gadgets, and superhero gadgets take things over the top. Who was the absolute king of superhero gadgets? That's right, Batman! Batman not only had great tools, but he was also the first superhero to have a secret compound, the legendary Batcave. He was also the first ordinary man to become a superhero—well, if stinking rich is ordinary. He trained hard, wore a really cool suit, drove a cool car, and had a boy wonder living with him. Hmm? But the kink with superheroes didn't stop with millionaire playboys.

MAN-TASTIC FACT

William Marston (and his wife) created the first polygraph to use blood pressure as a means of telling the truth. Marston also created Wonder Woman and gave her the Lasso of Truth to detect lies.

The first great female superhero is a man's dream, a perfectly gorgeous heroine with a love of bondage, submission, and the ladies. Wonder Woman was the creation of William Marston, a Harvard-trained lawyer and psychologist. Marston created Wonder Woman to show that a woman could be strong but also tender and loving, but he really liked the strong part. Wonder Woman was either tying people up or getting tied up in every issue, and she was also into spanking. Wonder Woman's catch phrase, "Suffering Sappho," pays homage to Sappho the poet, who was born on the island of Lesbos (you can see where this is going). Sappho's poetry gave rise to the term *lesbian*. Wonder Woman is getting hotter by the minute. Gorgeous and dressed in a fetish dream outfit, she was also

into S&M and possibly bisexuality . . . I can't wait for that movie to come out!

Marston even was quoted in a 1943 *Family Circle* article as saying, "Wonder Woman satisfies the subconscious, elaborately disguised desire of males to be mastered by a woman who loves them." The author of the article was a little-known writer named Olive Richard. Turns out Richard was only a pen name, and the writer's real name was Olive Byrne. She knew the good doctor much better than the article let on. Olive Byrne was Marston's former research assistant who ended up moving in with Marston and his wife. Olive and Marston's legal wife both shared Marston's bed and each bore him two children. Whether the two women were involved with each other is unknown, but after he died in 1947, they continued to live together for fifty years. Sounds like sometimes life really does imitate art.

MAN-TASTIC FACT

Superhero movies are standard summer blockbuster fare, and a two-hour movie in the theater uses about two miles of film. This is rapidly becoming a thing of the past as movie theaters switch to using digitally recorded movies on hard drives.

Top Ten Worst Manventions of All Time

1. Inflatable dart boards
2. Electric washcloths
3. Pop-up ads
4. Mullet hairdos
5. Solar-powered flashlights
6. Braille menus at the drive-through
7. Comb-overs
8. Recto rotors
9. Karaoke machines
10. Plus-sized Spandex workout gear

CHAPTER 2

SPORTS AND RECREATION:

TRASH TALK, JOCK STRAPS, AND SOME NICE, FRIENDLY COMPETITION

INSIDE THIS CHAPTER YOU WILL FIND:

- ☑ MMA AND UFC
- ☑ GOLF CARTS WITH BUILT-IN BEER COOLERS
- ☑ JOCK STRAPS AND CUPS
- ☑ SURFBOARDS, HANGING TEN, AND KOOK CORDS
- ☑ SHIN GUARDS AND HARD TACKLES
- ☑ BAGGY-ASS BASKETBALL SHORTS
- ☑ CLEATS, SPIKES, AND TRACTION
- ☑ THE SHOT CLOCK
- ☑ THE PENALTY BOX
- ☑ BMX AND MOUNTAIN BIKES

Men love the thrill of battle and will at least attempt to turn anything into a game—and yes, we mean anything. We bet, we trash talk, and we love to compete. We even trash talk when we are talking about "our team." Do any of you own a franchise? Yeah, me neither, but it doesn't matter. We will always be emotionally tied to *our* team and *our* players. And, in a world where we can change channels two thousand times an hour, it's comforting to know that we'll always be able to find some channel showing men competing for physical domination, even if the domination only involves something low key like bowling. So put on your jock and let's examine the man-sized world of sports and recreation.

MMA AND UFC

Mixed martial arts (MMA) has grabbed the sport's world by the tail in the last few years, but its roots are much older. Let's face it, men love bragging rights and have been fighting for them for thousands of years. MMA has just added a sense of legitimacy to what most of us did in elementary school. Now, the toughest and meanest kid on the playground has a chance to become a world superstar just by doing what he does best: fighting. And if that's not hard core, I don't know what is.

MMA had its organized beginnings in the ancient Olympic games in 648 B.C. as a sport called *Pankration,* which was essentially organized street fighting. Competitors would fight naked and pretty much anything went. Now naked man-wrestling may not be your

MAN-TASTIC FACT

In the early days of boxing, groups of fighters would barnstorm from town to town and challenge local fighters. Spectators would hold a ring of rope in a rough circle and any challenger could "throw his hat into the ring" to fight. As the number of fans grew, the fighters drove four stakes into the ground to hold the ropes. The square enclosure is still called a ring today.

MAN-DATE

The Gracies were first noticed in the United States in 1989, when Rorion Gracie was interviewed for *Playboy* magazine. Gracie claimed that he was the baddest man on the planet and issued the Gracie challenge. The family then came to the United States, and MMA exploded on the scene.

thing, but the ancient Greeks loved it—and let's be honest, you have to be secure in your manhood to get down and dirty with a naked dude.

MMA gained legitimacy in Brazil in the 1900s. The legendary Gracie family was behind this surge. Japanese master Mitsuyo Maeda taught Carlos Gracie the Japanese arts of judo and jujitsu and brought these previously hidden Japanese arts into the West. Gracie soon opened a gym and started training others—and charging them gobs of cash. To popularize his gym, Carlos issued the Gracie challenge. He put ads in the newspaper to challenge any fighters with his Brazilian form of jujitsu. Judo and jujitsu use leverage more than strength, so little fighters (the underdogs) still had a chance at a win. The matches were soon being held in large futbol stadiums throughout Brazil. Gracie and his brothers beat wrestlers, boxers, and karate experts. Some of the Gracie kids brought the sport to the United States in the 1990s.

The first Ultimate Fighting Championship (UFC), the Super Bowl of MMA, took place in 1993. Royce Gracie was the first champion, and he won by beating fighters who were much bigger than he. Any of the Gracies probably could have won, but Royce was chosen because he was the smallest and the family wanted to prove a point. The first UFC matches had no time limits, no judges, and almost no rules. It was literally a blood sport. This attracted interested viewers, but it also attracted politicians who lined up to stop these blood matches. Fortunately, a little marketing savvy swooped in to save the MMA.

The brash and sometimes offensive Dana White stepped in and became president in charge of the day-to-day operations of the UFC after White's childhood friend bought the organization. White instituted time limits, judges, and tapouts (though submissions had always been part of the sport). The sport took off and reached its lofty status as one of the world's most popular spectator sports—and one of mankind's favorite manventions.

GOLF CARTS WITH BUILT-IN BEER COOLERS

Men love golf. Chasing that little white ball around a huge, green course gives us immense pleasure. But walking around that huge, green course chasing after the ball just isn't any fun. Enter the golf cart—that wonderful manvention that allows us to wander near and far in search of stray balls.

MAN-TASTIC FACT

Peachtree City, a suburb of Atlanta, Georgia, has over ninety miles of golf cart paths. The local high school even has a parking lot for golf carts.

MAN-DATE

The first rules of golf were written in 1774. They included the rule that the ball must be teed up one club length from the hole. Separate tee boxes weren't created until later.

During World War II, gas was rationed and people needed another way to get around, so Merle Williams built an electric cart for his wife to drive around when she needed to run errands. The idea took off and Williams soon started selling electric carts to many people. When the war ended, he saw an opportunity and jumped at it. In 1951, he sold the first cart to a golf course and history was made. Soon thousands of men were found driving around the golf course chasing little white balls. Williams's Marketeer Company was eventually joined in making carts by Club Car, E-Z-GO, Yamaha, and even Harley-Davidson (talk about playing some hard-core golf).

Golf carts have come a long way since World War II. Now, you can get them with four-wheel drive and in any color you want, but my favorites are the ones with built-in coolers. Cold beer at the lift of a lid sounds like the good life to me. And the way many of us play, beer is a welcome addition to the game.

Golf carts are increasingly found off of the golf course (and not only on the chase for errant balls). Go to any retirement community. Golf carts. Go to any beachfront community. Golf carts. Go to any race-car race. Golf carts. Go to a movie set. Golf carts. It seems like golf carts are the primary means of transportation if you have money—unless you are a professional golfer. Pro golfers, by rule, must walk. Of course, they have a pack mule (called a caddie) to carry their bags.

Golf carts are a great manvention that serve their adoring public well. They allow us to chase wayward balls. They allow us to take stuff to the beach when we are on vacation. They allow movie stars to travel the set in style. But most of all, they allow the average golfer to take a load off—and keep their beer cold. It just doesn't get any better than that.

MAN-TASTIC FACT

One of the major manventions in golf was the gutta-percha ball. The hard rubber gutta sap could easily be formed into hard, long-lasting golf balls. This style of golf ball was the most common from 1848 to the early twentieth century. By the way, gutta-percha is still used by most dentists. It is heated up and placed inside your tooth during a root canal.

JOCK STRAPS AND CUPS

We're not talking about the World Cup, Lord Stanley's Cup, or even a Dixie cup. We are talking about the save-your-nuts cup. If you've ever played a sport—or been kicked in the nuts during a bar fight—you know that the cup and the jock strap are integral parts of saving the male anatomy. After all, we men must protect our twigs and our berries.

> **MAN-DATE**
>
> In 2005, Bike Athletic (now a division of Russell Athletic) made their 350-millionth jock strap.

The jock strap grew out of loincloths and codpieces. Loincloths have been used ever since the cavemen days. After all, you don't want your meat pole flopping while chasing a woolly mammoth. Leather was later added for more protection (think gladiators here). Codpieces started as a flap that wrapped from the bottom and tied at the top, which made using a Dark Ages urinal a wee more convenient. It didn't take men long to stuff their codpieces to show their manhood. Steel codpieces became the norm for battle (and still exist today in certain underground S&M clubs), and the lowly codpiece began to slowly evolve into the jock of today that we all know and love.

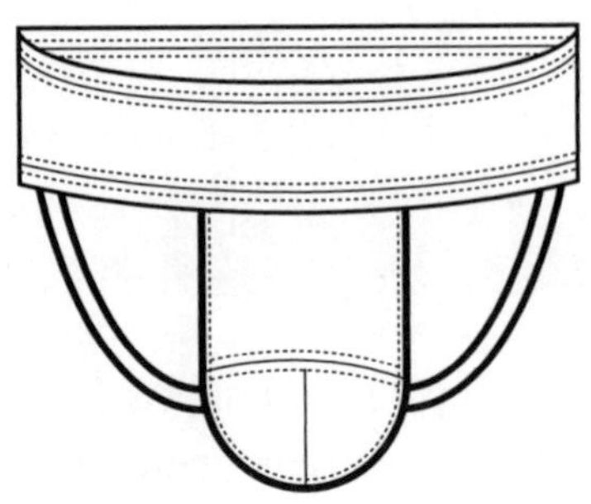

The modern jock strap was invented by Charles Bennett in 1874 and was called the Bike Jockey Strap. The Bike Web Company was formed soon after to make these itchy undergarments. Men no longer had to worry about flopping around when they were riding a bike or playing a sport. The cup was added in the 1920s as a modern day version of the codpiece to protect the family jewels during baseball, cricket, mixed martial arts, and many other sports. Millions of game-playing men are thankful for the lowly jock—and so are their wives.

MAN-TASTIC FACT

King Tut was buried with over 140 loincloths. Wonder what he planned on doing in the afterlife?

SURFBOARDS, HANGING TEN, AND KOOK CORDS

Even if you have never ridden a wave, surfboards hold an incredible allure. They have been glorified in movies, song, and pop culture, and surfboard lingo probably kept many of you communicating when you were in college. Maybe we ought to keep the tradition alive and liven up our next board meeting by greeting our boss with a little healthy surf slang, "Yo dude! When the board meeting starting? Totally tubular!" The surfboard earned its place on the manvention list in the 1960s and remains enshrined there today.

Surfing is often called "the sport of kings," and there is a lot of truth to that. We may think of surfing as an activity done by a blonde, tanned, California teen, but that isn't how it began. Surfing actually started in the Pacific islands of Tahiti, Polynesia, and

Hawaii. Pacific chiefs had to demonstrate their strength and agility on the hardwood boards of the day. Some of the boards were up to eighteen feet long and weighed as much as 200 pounds. The rest of the world didn't learn about surfing until 1779 when Captain James Cook's journals were published. His tales of the daring men riding the waves captivated readers, but there were a few people who were not so excited.

Missionaries who arrived at the islands in the 1820s saw surfing as a sport of heathens. They might have hated the decadence of bronze, naked men surfing, or they may have frowned upon the betting on the size of the wave or the length of the ride that was common among the surf watchers. Either way, surfing was nearly extinct by the end of the 1800s. Only a few native kings kept alive this Polynesian tradition. It would take an unlikely duo to make surfing a common theme in music and movies.

Two surf legends toured the world and shared surfing at the same time. The first surf ambassador was Irish-Hawaiian George Freeth. Imagine having that ancestry! You'd surf all day and drink all night. Legendary writer Jack London brought Freeth into the limelight when Freeth taught London how to surf. London also wrote a piece on "surf-bathing" for the *Ladies Home Companion*. In 1907, Freeth asked London for a letter of recommendation and took off to California.

> ### *MAN-TASTIC FACT*
>
> **Surf leashes were originally called "kook cords" by veteran surfers who believed you should pay the price for a wipeout with a long swim spent chasing your board.**

A local newspaper ran an article on the surfer riding the waves in Venice that drew the interest of real estate and trolley car magnate Henry Huntington, who had his own beachfront property to sell. He put Freeth on the payroll and heavily advertised "the man who can walk on water." Freeth's twice daily surf shows drew interest in Redondo Beach and helped create the California beach lifestyle. Freeth was also the first paid lifeguard in the United States and developed the torpedo-style life buoy that is still used today.

The other early surf god was Hawaiian Olympic swimming champion Duke Kahanamoku. Duke toured the United States and Australia giving swimming and surfing lessons from 1915 through the 1920s. He usually rode a sixteen-foot hardwood board without a fin (fins and fiberglass came later). His bronze chiseled physique and fame elevated surfing and, with his five Olympic medals, Duke was a fabulous ambassador for the sport. Soon surfers no longer looked Polynesian; they looked like the prototypical sun-bleached California male. And, as surfing caught on, shorter boards, fiberglass, fins, and leashes all made the sport easier and safer for the masses.

Surfboards and the surf lifestyle eventually led to the formation and music of the Beach Boys and all of their imitators.

Surfing also led to countless beach-inspired movies, including *Gidget, Beach Blanket Bingo, The Ghost in the Invisible Bikini,* and *Psycho Beach Party*. Surfing even allowed Keanu Reeves to look like a real actor in *Point Break*. And if Keanu Reeves can look cool surfing, so can any guy out there.

> ***MAN-TASTIC FACT***
>
> **The letters SOS mean nothing, but they are easy to remember. In Morse code, the letters are three dashes, three dots, and three dashes.**

SHIN GUARDS AND HARD TACKLES

Men love the thrill of victory, but we really hate the agony we're in after a hard-won game of soccer. Enter the alternatively loved and hated shin guard. They are uncomfortable, but by God they save us from pain. And anything that can do that is a great man-vention in my book.

The first shin guards were actually cut-down cricket pads for the shins that were passed over to soccer in 1874. Today's shin guards are lighter and more comfortable than ever before due to advances in science, but we still hate to wear them unless it's absolutely necessary. Which

it so often is. You see, we have no muscle on the shin to save it from damage, so a little padding is nice. This was especially important in the early days of soccer when there weren't any referees. Each team would supply an umpire and fouling was unheard of. Of course, gentlemen would never foul to gain an advantage (and back then soccer was for gentlemen). I guess I never played with gentlemen, because in our games everything is legal until you get carded.

MAN-DATE

In the World Cup of 1966, Rudolf Krietlein, a German referee, kicked an Argentinean off the field for arguing. He later issued a warning to an Englishman for nasty play. Unfortunately, none of the three spoke the same language, which inevitably led to some issues. Ken Aston, the head of referees at the 1966 World Cup, drove home thinking about a solution to the language barrier. At a traffic light, it hit him: yellow for caution and red for stop. Red and yellow cards were first used in the 1970 World Cup.

BAGGY-ASS BASKETBALL SHORTS

Men like comfort and style, and in today's basketball shorts we get both. Gone are the days of the nut-hugging shorts of the Hoosiers, Larry Bird, and Magic Johnson. They have been replaced with thigh-length, baggy drawers, and we owe it all to a couple of basketball legends.

Michael Jordan is a basketball god, and he wore a pair of his college nut-hugging shorts under his uniform as a good luck charm. Well, if you are going to wear two pairs of shorts, the outside pair needs to be bigger. He also liked to have something to grab when he leaned over to catch his breath, and the long shorts were born. Since he was a b-ball god, aspiring hoopsters copied the look, but it took a legendary college team to make basketball shorts even baggier.

The "Fab Five" University of Michigan team in 1991–92 and 1992–93 may have been one of the greatest collections of talent to ever lace up their sneakers for the same university at the same time. And the five players wore not only baggy shorts but loose-fitting tops, and the look caught on with all of the basketball-playing world. Of course, the Fab Five also wore black socks with their basketball sneakers. This look also caught on, at least with old men. Just head to the local retirement home and you can see that little bit of fashion splendor as the old men shuffle into the dining hall.

MAN-TASTIC FACT

Baggy shorts aren't new to sports. The West Bromwich Albion Football Club is named the Baggies after the baggy shorts they wore in the early 1900s.

Fashion tends to run in cycles, so maybe nut-huggers will make a comeback, but I doubt it. For men, comfort will always trump fashion, so baggy-ass shorts are here to stay—for men anyway. Tight shorts on the right woman is a totally different story . . .

CLEATS, SPIKES, AND TRACTION

MAN-DATE

The familiar Nike swoosh logo was commissioned from a graphic design student for $35 in 1971. In 1983, Nike gave the former student an undisclosed amount of stock as a way of saying thank you.

The first time a boy plays an outdoor game in PE wearing sneakers and falls on his ass when he can't stop, he realizes that life could be better. There has to be a better way. Fortunately there is a better way via a pair of fancy shoes called cleats. Since we love sports—and anything that makes sports better—we worship cleats as one of the world's greatest manventions.

The first documented pair of sports cleats were owned by a rich, fat kid, none other than King Henry the Eighth of the six wives' fame. He paid his shoemaker to make him a pair of soccer boots that would make him better than anyone else on the field. The boots were ankle high, made of leather, and thicker than the current styles of shoes. He paid his cobbler the equivalent of about $225 for his pair. Sports shoes were expensive for men even in 1526.

Over the next 300 years the game of soccer (football to everyone except us Americans) became more organized. In industrial England, some of the first organized games were between competing factory teams. The men would play in their work boots, leather high tops with steel toes. They hammered steel studs or tacks into the bottom to increase traction, and this is the way

MAN-DATE

In 1948, Adolf and Rudolf split up the Dassler Shoe Company after years of sibling rivalry. Adolf (also called Adi) formed Adidas. Brother Rudolf formed the Puma shoe company and the rivalry continued. Even though the brothers are dead their companies still battle for shoe supremacy.

cleats were made until the early 1900s when the Dasslers changed the game.

In 1924, Adolf and Rudolf Dassler created the Dassler Brothers Shoe Company and designed a shoe with replaceable, nailed studs that could be changed based on field conditions. As World War II ended and air travel played a more important role in competitive soccer, cleats took front stage. The South American teams wore low-cut shoes made from thin leather. This gave them more ball control. Most companies soon followed suit creating a slipper style shoe with cleats on the bottom.

In America, baseball was king and football was starting to explode. Baseball cleats were work shoes that had metal spikes placed on the bottom for traction on the base paths. These metal spikes also became weapons in the hands of players like Ty Cobb. It sure was easier to steal bases if you slid in with your spikes high. But, while baseball cleats stayed pretty much constant over the years until the advent of plastic molded spikes, American football cleats continued to evolve.

As American football grew in popularity, the shoes became more sophisticated. High-top work boots with nailed studs were slowly phased out in favor of screwable studs. John Riddell was a high school football coach in Evanston, Illinois. His team's shoes had nailed-in cleats on the bottom. When the weather soured, he would run to his cobbler to change all of the players' cleats. However, since Riddell's high school team used the same cobbler as Northwestern University, Riddell's shoes often took a backseat and occasionally weren't done by game time, so he had to find another way. He designed a cleat that could be screwed in by anyone who needed a change. The screwable stud was born for football. In 1927, Riddell quit teaching to make shoes and sporting goods full time. His shoes aren't worn much anymore, but Riddell is the largest maker of football helmets in the world.

Cleats are a given in today's field sports, but they're no longer the sole property of rich fat kids; they are owned by all of us testosterone-driven athletes. We take cleats for granted now when we play, but we need to pay homage to the creators of these shoes that made sports competition even more fierce.

MAN-DATE

Although some form of shoelaces have existed for thousands of years, the idea of using a lace and holes in the shoes was first thought up by Harvy Kennedy in 1790. Prior to laces, most shoes had buckles or were some form of sandals.

THE SHOT CLOCK

Let's face it, men are an impatient lot. We want our sports played at a fast and furious rate. In fact, the only place we want the action to slow down is in the bedroom. In sports, to speed up play, we have the beloved shot clock. In the NBA, players have twenty-four seconds to make a shot before the buzzer goes off and possession is given to the opposing team. In the NFL, teams have forty seconds before they're forced to run their next play.

The shot clock first appeared in the NBA in the days of nut-hugging shorts (way back in the 1950s). Basketball in those days was pretty boring. Games would end up 19–18, as opposed to scores that typically reach triple digits today. Back then, once a team got the lead they would slow the game way down. Most men are all in favor of bending the rules, and then the rules allowed players to delay, delay, delay. The Four Corners offense was legendary in its ability to slow down the game. A team would put a man in each of the four corners of the offensive zone, then they would just run and pass, keeping the ball away from the other team. There was no need to even shoot the ball. After all, the other team can't win if they never get a shot off. In 1954, that all changed in the NBA as a twenty-four-second shot clock was created by the

MAN-DATE

The Syracuse Nationals won the NBA championship the year after the shot clock became law. Do you remember the Syracuse Nationals? They moved to Philadelphia in 1963 and became the 76ers.

owner of the Syracuse Nationals. Many experts say the shot clock saved the NBA by making the games faster.

Today, college and pro hoops as well as pro lacrosse use the shot clock, and pro football and pro baseball use a play clock, which is essentially the same thing. Slow just isn't good when you're talking sports, unless you're talking golf. Then you want to take your time and get it right. But for the rest of these sports, anything that keeps the game moving is a great manvention.

THE PENALTY BOX

The manliest way to get punished in sports is the penalty box; it's a kind of timeout for grownups. The penalty box is famous in hockey. You're banished to the box where you sit for two minutes for a minor infraction and five minutes for a major rule break, and your team continues to play while you do your time. However, penalty boxes are also used in other sports like rugby, water polo, lacrosse, and roller derby. Maybe this grown-up form of timeout should extend to other venues. Make an accounting mistake, you get ten minutes in the corner holding a piece of paper to the wall using only your nose. Make a hard slide in baseball, the next inning your team only gets eight players in the field. Tackle violently in football, you only get ten players the next play. Throw an elbow in basketball, play with four players the next two minutes.

For married men, the penalty box already exists. It is called the doghouse, which is where you end up when you screw up. The doghouse usually involves sleeping on the couch and lots of groveling to get back in your wife's good graces. Maybe hockey players should have to grovel to the refs to get back in the game. "I promise I will never slash another player. I promise I won't hook another player, please just let me back in to play." On second thought though, groveling is not manly, especially when it comes to sports. After all, it's not like you want to sleep with the ref.

> **MAN-TASTIC FACT**
>
> In rugby, the penalty box is lovingly called the sin bin.

BMX AND MOUNTAIN BIKES

Men like to get dirty and we love the outdoors. One continually evolving manvention that combines the two is the bicycle—mountain bikes and BMX bikes to be specific. The fact that we might end up going to the emergency room for x-rays just adds to the allure.

Bikes have been around forever (well, since 1817), but today mountain bikes rule the man world. Mountain bikes grew out of the funky, fat-tire bikes (called cruisers) that showed up in the 1950s and 1960s. Every kid's bike has gone off road at some point in time (whether you wanted it to or not), and fat tires made that off-road trip a little more comfortable (at least until you wiped out). My off-road biking experiences always ended at the bottom of Death Race Hill with me bent around a tree, but I sure appreciated the smooth ride I got on the way down.

Apparently I had the right idea because mountain bike racing started in Marin, California, when a bunch of amateurs started racing jury-rigged cruisers down an old fire trail in a race soon to be known as the Repack. It was so named because after each downhill ride you would have to repack your wheel hubs because of the abuse. The average bike just wasn't designed for this type of ride, but it was so much fun that men started designing bikes that could handle it. Today, shocks, suspension, high-tech materials, and crazy frame geometry have made mountain biking even more manly. They have also probably saved us a few trips to the emergency room, but not every trip; the potential for disaster is part of what makes it fun.

MAN-TASTIC FACT

Mountain biking was added to the Olympics in 1996 in Atlanta, Georgia. The woman's winner was Paola Pezzo, an Italian who liked tight spandex and showing her cleavage to the crowd.

Independent of mountain biking, which was primarily for adults, grew the sport of BMX (short for

Bicycle Moto-Cross). BMX also started in California in the 1970s as teens took their bikes and modified them to ride on off-road motorcycle courses. The action is fast and furious. BMX goes balls-to-the-wall with all riders on the track together. Crashes are common, and kicking the other riders is not unheard of; you win by any means necessary.

> ***Man-tastic Fact***
>
> **Even if you don't ride, you can still worship mountain biking with a Fat Tire beer.**

Freestyle BMX grew as kids started experimenting with their bikes and figured out how to do tricks. Freestyle is now an X Games favorite. Most freestyle bikes have twenty-inch rims (like the bikes you rode when you were twelve) but are heavily modified with pegs on the wheels and extra-strong frames. Freestylers compete in street (using railings, stairs, and so on), park (using skateboard park mainstays like bowls), and vert (using a tall half-pipe to get up in the air) events—each one more testosterone-filled than the one before.

TOP TEN TACKIEST TV MANVENTIONS

1. Hair in a Can Spray
2. The Clapper
3. Chia Pets
4. Ginsu knives
5. Popeil Pocket Fisherman
6. Inside-the-Shell Egg Scrambler
7. The Flowbee
8. Mr. Microphone
9. ShamWow
10. Battery-operated battery chargers

CHAPTER 3

FOOD AND DRINK:

WHO DOESN'T LOVE A HOT POCKET AND AN ICE-COLD COORS LIGHT?

INSIDE THIS CHAPTER YOU WILL FIND:

- ☑ TABASCO SAUCE
- ☑ HOT POCKETS AND MICROWAVE POPCORN
- ☑ ICEMAKERS
- ☑ GATORADE
- ☑ RED BULL
- ☑ CUBAN CIGARS
- ☑ VENDING MACHINES
- ☑ BOTTLE OPENERS
- ☑ COLD-ACTIVATED BEER BOTTLES
- ☑ THE KFC DOUBLE DOWN
- ☑ JACK DANIELS
- ☑ KINGSFORD CHARCOAL, LIGHTER FLUID, AND GIANT FLAMES
- ☑ CHIMNEY STARTERS, BBQ TONGS, AND TELESCOPING FORKS
- ☑ GAS GRILLS
- ☑ BEER (NEED I SAY MORE?)
- ☑ BEER HELMETS
- ☑ MR. COFFEE AND THE KEURIG

Men love to eat, drink, and be merry. And if we aren't feeling merry, we just like to drink. Luckily, there are some amazing manventions that help us do just that. We have our fill of electrolyte drinks, energy drinks, and alcoholic drinks, but man cannot live by drink alone—even though many may try. Fortunately there are some genius products out there that make eating even more manly. So, grab a pint and let's delve into the world of food and drink manventions.

TABASCO SAUCE

In the category of extreme manventions, nothing foots the bill like hot sauce, the hotter the better. The perfect sauce is something that will make your eyeballs sweat and that you have to sign a waiver to try. There are dozens of hot sauces to choose from, but we owe the most famous brand to a man broken by the Civil War.

Edmund McIlhenny was working as a New Orleans banker in the mid-1800s when he received a gift that would change mankind forever. A soldier returning from the Mexican-American War gave him some dried peppers and implored him to use them in cooking. They were fabulous! McIlhenny kept some of the seeds and planted them on his plantation. Then, a nasty little war broke out in the 1860s and McIlhenny and his good Southern family fled to Texas where they stayed until the hostilities ended.

When the family returned the mansion was ruined, but McIlhenny's loss became mankind's gain. The only thing remaining on the plantation was the crop of peppers, and McIlhenny quickly turned this into cash. He mixed his peppers with vinegar and salt and made a tasty little hot sauce that he bottled in old cologne bottles and quickly sold to spice-loving men everywhere. Tabasco Pepper Sauce was born! McIlhenny patented his ingredients and later trademarked the Tabasco name to fend off an ex-employee hell-bent on making his own fortune off hot sauce. The green wax tops were added as a way to seal the bottle.

MAN-TASTIC FACT

Each bottle of Tabasco sauce contains 720 drops of the wonderful elixir.

Ever since Tabasco came onto the market, men have been putting the hot sauce on anything they can get their hands on—even liquor. Fernand "Pete" Periot, an American bartender in Paris, added a little Tabasco sauce to tomato sauce and vodka and made the first Bloody Mary. In 1934, he moved to New York and refined his famous drink with a dash of Worcestershire, lemon-lime, and horseradish. The drink was a success. And many men use a Blood Mary to ward off one of man's least favorite things ever, the hangover. You gotta love a manvention that works as the hair of the dog. Bring on the heat!

MAN-DATE

In a stroke of marketing genius, the McIlhenny company used the Vietnam War to help spread the love of hot sauce. Tiny bottles were wrapped with cookbooks full of ideas to spice up those oh-so-tasty C-ration meals. The soldiers loved it.

HOT POCKETS AND MICROWAVE POPCORN

Men are impatient, especially when we're hungry. We want what we want and we want it now. Enter one of the best manventions ever: the microwave oven. Anything that can give you fast food in your dorm, office, or even your own kitchen in two minutes or less is pretty spectacular. And to think we owe the pleasure of nuked food to a melted candy bar . . .

The year was 1946. The place was some research lab in California. The person was Dr. Percy Spencer, a geeky-ass scientist. As he toured one of the labs, he stepped in front of a magnetron (a power tube that creates radar waves). He felt a burning sensation and realized that the chocolate bar in his pocket had melted. The race was on to see what else he could nuke. He eventually figured out how to cook almost anything with his magnetron. Raytheon released the first microwave in 1947, but it didn't sell well due to its large size; it was as large as a modern day kegerator (refrigerator for you non-drinkers). It took advances in electronics to create the food-nuking machine that men love.

After the microwave shrunk to its current size, the race was on to create fast food for men. One all-time man fave is the Hot Pocket. Really, there's almost no food product that's more amazing. Just pop a Hot Pocket into the microwave and two minutes later you have a hot collection of dough, meat, and cheese. The secret is the crisping sleeve. The sleeve has metal in it (I know, you're not supposed to put metal in a microwave, but this is perfectly safe) that converts the microwave energy into heat at the surface of the Hot Pocket. This results in a somewhat browned crust for the Hot Pocket. Of course, consuming Hot Pockets may lead to extended bouts on the throne due to their ability to make us—or at least our bowels—move, but it is definitely

MAN-TASTIC FACT

The first microwave oven was five and a half feet tall and weighed 750 pounds. This might be an ideal size for a sumo wrestler, but it was not a handy kitchen gadget.

worth it. Microwave popcorn is another man fave. Pop it in and five minutes later you have a bag of preflavored, puffed-up, superheated starch. Yum. We can even heat up entire meals in the microwave.

So don't think men can't cook. We can. We just need an open flame—or a microwave oven.

ICEMAKERS

An often overlooked manvention that most of us dearly love is the icemaker. Sure, it's just in your fridge. You probably don't pay much attention to it, but just try to imagine a world without ice at your fingertips. Warm soda and warm bourbon are just not good for the soul. Men want cold drinks in the summer. We want to keep beer cold at a tailgate party. We want to enjoy figure skating year round . . . just kidding! Wanted to see if you were paying attention. Guys only watch figure skating because women make us. But icemakers really do deserve their place on the manvention list.

> **MAN-TASTIC FACT**
>
> A Zamboni machine travels about three miles during an average hockey game.

Men love making a dollar off of others. We admire entrepreneurs, guys like Frederic Tudor. Tudor lived in the Northeast and basically had free ice for much of the year. Hell, the stuff just grows on the surface of every pond in New England, why not just cut up the stuff and sell it to others? Tudor cut up the ice, loaded it in ships, and shipped it to places like the Caribbean and India where he sold it for cold, hard cash. He also sold ice locally to men who were too lazy to go cut their own and became a millionaire. Ice houses started appearing anyplace that there was ice as more men jumped on the "sell something we got for free" bandwagon.

However, there were two disadvantages to the ice-cutting business: 1) Cutting ice out of a pond was hard work, and 2) you actually had to have ice to cut. So men started searching for a way to make ice. Guys like Dr. John Gorrie came to the rescue. Gorrie was a Florida physician who needed ice to cool down his feverish patients. He developed one of the first patented mechanical icemakers to help out the hospital. Gorrie didn't get rich, but he did lead the way for all of the many mechanical icemakers that followed. And thank God he did! Men love the new ice age. What could be better than a scotch on the rocks, cold beer, and a sixty-four-ounce tanker-sized soda?

MAN-DATE

In 1927, an enterprising employee at the Southland Ice Company began selling milk, eggs, and bread right off the loading dock on Sundays and evenings (when traditional grocery stores were closed). All of the Southland Ice stores quickly started selling foods at convenient times and the convenience store was born. Today the former ice company is known as 7-Eleven.

GATORADE

Men like to win. And whether we're crushing our friends on the tennis court or on the b-ball court, we'll take any advantage we can get. One such advantage—Gatorade—showed up in the 1960s in Florida.

Gatorade is the king of the electrolyte drinks, but it started out as the king of the University of Florida practice field. In 1965, a UF assistant football coach asked Dr. Robert Cade, an electrolyte specialist when most men didn't know what the hell an electrolyte was, why the players would sweat so much during practice but couldn't urinate later. Cade and his team got permission from an admittedly clueless Ray Graves (head football coach) to test the freshmen football players with different sports drinks. He combined water, salt, and sugar to keep the players hydrated and full of energy. The problem was that the concoction tasted disgusting. At his wife's suggestion, he added some lemon juice

MAN-DATE

In the 1980s, Coca-Cola released an advertising poster in South Australia that turned out to be one of the most collectible ever, but not for the right reasons. Seems the artist hid a picture of a penis aimed at a woman's face profile in ice cubes in the picture. An Australian noticed the hidden artwork when it was blown up and put on the side of a truck. The artist was fired and sued over the incident. Coke tried to recall all the artwork, which was by then plastered everywhere.

and Gatorade was born. The freshman team began to dominate the varsity second team in hot scrimmages, and Graves used Gatorade the next Saturday to beat LSU in 102-degree heat. The legend was born.

Cade eventually sold the rights to Stokely-Van Camp and the marketing frenzy began—and so did the legal battles. In 1973, a deal was reached: Cade and his team and UF would split the royalties. UF receives about $11 million a year from the sale of Gatorade. Sports drinks are here to stay and now come in many flavors and varieties, but Gatorade was the first and is still the undisputed leader of the sports drink market.

RED BULL

Long drive ahead? Grab a Red Bull. Need to pull an all-nighter? Grab a Red Bull. Need to work a double shift at work? Grab a Red Bull. With all the stuff we have to get done in such little time, energy drinks sales have skyrocketed over the last twenty years—and Red Bull is the best energy drink on the market. It pretty much cranks us up to the point that we can do anything . . . and we Westerners owe it all to jet lag.

Blue-collar workers in Southeast Asia have been consuming noncarbonated energy drinks since the 1960s. The drinks were readily consumed by truck drivers, farmers, and factory workers to amp them up for a long haul. But it took a marketing person to turn Red Bull into a college-student favorite. Dietrich Mateschitz, an Austrian toothpaste marketer, ran across Krating Daeng (a.k.a. Red Bull) while on a business trip in Thailand. Mateschitz was suffering from a really bad case of jet lag, so when he saw workers consuming the drink he tried one. Goodbye jet lag! He finagled a deal for the world marketing rights for Red Bull and the rest is history. He marketed the drinks to adrenalin-loving men in the Western world and sales took off. Red Bull is the number one energy drink in the world.

While Gatorade and the electrolyte drinks rely on sugar, water, and salt, energy drinks rely on chemicals (plus sugar and water). The number one chemical for staying awake is caffeine, and the amount of caffeine found in an energy drink dwarfs the amount you'd find in a cup of coffee. They also may contain brain-wakening stuff like ginseng, acai, vitamin B, ginkgo, and guarana (which contains even more caffeine). Millions of jacked-up men love their Red Bull, but they love it even more when it's dressed up for an evening out.

If you have been to a bar in the last twenty years, you have probably dropped a bomb, a Jägerbomb, that is. Jägerbombs are created when a shot of Jägermeister is dropped into a glass of Red Bull. The concoction counters alcohol's

> ***MAN-TASTIC FACT***
>
> **The Red Bull Stratos team is planning a parachute jump from 120,000 feet. From that height, the space diver (Felix Baumgartner) would break the sound barrier.**

depressing quality with a pure shot of energy. And that pure shot of energy leads to more of the black bombs—or perhaps to a Jägertrain, which is created when glasses of Red Bull are lined up with shots of Jäger resting between the glasses. Push over the first shot glass and you have the college equivalent to alcoholic dominoes. And alcoholic dominoes lead to the worst manvention ever: the hangover.

CUBAN CIGARS

The cigar is a manvention that is practically crying out to be enjoyed. The sweet taste of a cigar to an aficionado is like ice cream to a fat man, something to be savored. After all, what's more manly than smoking a celebratory cigar with your friends when a baby is born or when you get that big promotion at work. Cigars represent prosperity and good fortune, and they also allow you to annoy a few people around you with that wonderful smoke.

Cigars are at least a thousand years old; Mayan pots have been dug up showing men smoking what appears to be cigars. Native and Central Americans cherished tobacco so much that it was carried as a form of currency, and rolled tobacco leaves were a great way to barter for your life with those friendly cannibals you just met. Prior to fears of lung cancer, people used to smoke with each other as a sign of friendship or celebration (and still do, just not as often). It was probably an act of friendship that first introduced cigars to Columbus and his crew. Let's see, Native Americans gave Columbus gold, silver, tomatoes, chili peppers, and tobacco to take back to the Old World. Chris gave the Native Americans small pox in return. Fair trade? Not so much.

The heyday of cigars had to be the Civil War, when practically every Rebel or Yank of note was seen smoking a cigar. And almost all old houses had a smoking room where the menfolk would retire after dinner for an adult beverage and a smoke. The best cigars were (and still are) made in Central America and the Caribbean. In fact, many say that the best cigars are made in Cuba. Unfortunately, Cuban cigars are also illegal in the United States. In 1962, JFK established a trade embargo with Cuba over Russian missiles. That embargo has kept men from getting the goods ever since. However, even JFK himself knew that Cubans were the best cigar on the market. He reportedly told his press secretary to buy as many as he could get before the stores sold out. Cuban cigars are still available in the United States, but you have to go through some pretty sketchy channels to get them. They're also very expensive, but many men have no problem forking over their hard-earned cash for a perfect cigar.

Cigar smokers also get really neat toys, and what guy doesn't love a fun gadget. First are the

MAN-TASTIC FACT

The Marlboro Man was an advertising icon from the 1950s who puffed his way through ads until cigarette advertising on television was banned in the 1970s. The actor who portrayed the Marlboro Man, perhaps not unexpectedly, died of lung cancer.

really cool blowtorch lighters. Men love fire, and not much looks cooler than the pencil-thin blue flame of a torch lighter. Second, cigar lovers get pretty sweet cigar cutters that are perfect for cigars or for an emergency circumcision. Hopefully, you never find yourself in that situation.

Cigar sales have rebounded in the past twenty years. Men are willing to risk a little for the taste of a good stogie and the camaraderie that comes from smoking with other men. After all, it is a great way to unwind and spread a little peace. And if your wife or girlfriend complains, just tell her that you're getting in touch with your Native American ancestors.

VENDING MACHINES

Men love convenience. We don't want to wait for anything, and we get really impatient at any delay. Enter the vending machine. Instantly, we can get everything we need, from sodas to condoms, with just a few falling coins, a perfect crisp paper money bill (don't even try to put in a dollar that's been balled up in your pocket; the result will just make you angry), or a swipe of a card. In some places, you can even use your cell phone.

Hero of Alexandria developed the earliest known vending machine in 215 B.C. These vending machines were placed at Egyptian temples and dispensed holy water to anyone willing to pay for it. His machine had a lever in it. When a coin fell onto that lever, water was dispensed until the coin slid off the lever and closed it. It was good enough for Egyptian gods, but it would take a couple of thousand years before the vending machine was good enough for the rest of us.

With the industrial age came all manner of moving machines invented to make modern man's life easier. The first modern vending machine was created in London in the 1880s to sell postcards. A few years later the first gum machines came onto the scene. These vending machines sold Tutti-Frutti gum and were placed on New York City subway platforms in 1888 by Thomas Adams. The ironic part is that Adams's rise as a gum maker was actually due to the influence of a hated enemy of the United States, Antonio López de Santa Anna. The conquering general at the Alamo, Santa Anna was exiled from Mexico after the Texans won the war. During his travels, he actually stayed with Adams at Adams's Staten Island home. Santa Anna was convinced a use could be found for chicle, a rubberlike substance derived from the sap of the sapodilla tree. Like many Mexicans (and the Mayans before that), he also chewed chicle. Adams tried to make toys, rain boots, and even tires out of the chicle with no success. Realizing that Santa Anna chewed the stuff, Adams set out to make gum. The Adams company today is owned by Cadbury and makes Chiclets gum, along with dozens of other sweets.

Candy-coated gumballs were added to vending machines in 1907, and many vending machine favorites were still to come. Soda was dispensed into a cup in the 1920s and in bottles and cans later. Cigarettes also joined the mix in the 1920s but since then have pretty much disappeared from machines in the United States. In addition, the single-cup coffee vending machine, a favorite of many workers, was invented after World War II.

Complete vending-machine restaurants were opened in the early part of the twentieth century. The most famous of these automats in the United States was Horn & Hardart. They served fresh food behind a sliding glass door that was opened by the proper coinage. In the 1940s and 1950s, they served over 500,000 customers daily in the Philadelphia and New York areas. The automat's decline in the United States coincided with the rise of fast food restaurants. Today, the Smithsonian has an elaborate thirty-five-foot section of the 1902 Horn & Hardart Automat from Philadelphia in its collection. Automats are still popular in several countries around the world, most notably the Netherlands.

> **MAN-TASTIC FACT**
>
> It is estimated that Japan has one vending machine for every twenty-three people. And you can buy anything from liquor to hot ramen noodles from vending machines. After food, one of the biggest sellers from Japanese vending machines is porn that you can pay for with your cell phone. Talk about convenience.

Every guy, from the hard-driving, hard-living man who lives on the road to the guy who just wants a snack during his lunch break, loves a good vending machine. How could we not love something that sells us everything from Coke to condoms for just the loose change rolling around in our cars. Sounds like a great manvention to me.

BOTTLE OPENERS

The bottle opener is the tool that men use more often than any other tool in their arsenal. After all, even if you're playing with your cordless drill, you'll probably pop open a brewskie as soon as you're finished up for the day—if not before. And you need a bottle opener to get to the object of your attention.

Bottle openers have a long and illustrious history. Pop-top cans and twist-off bottles may rule the world today, but that wasn't always the case. Early beer cans had a smooth top and needed to be opened by a triangular bottle opener called a *church key*. After all, if you want to go to heaven, you have to open the door. And heaven for most men equals beer. *Church keys*, bottle openers that looked like ornate church keys, have been around since 1898, but they weren't originally used to open beer bottles. Back in the day, most food came in cans (beer didn't), so the church key had a bent triangle point to pierce the cans on one end and had a crude can opener/bottle opener attached on the other end.

Beer first showed up in cans in 1935 just after Prohibition was repealed, and the church key found new purpose! The triangle end of the church key was the most important part in the early days. To get into the cans, drinkers would create two triangular Vs in the top of the can (opposite each other to

MAN-TASTIC FACT

Cenosillicaphobia is the fear of an empty glass. A standard U.S. keg will deliver 200 to 220 twelve-ounce beers to ward off this evil phobia.

let air in so the beer would pour out easily) and away they went. The other end of the church key was used to pop off the "crown cork" that is still in use to seal glass beer bottles today.

The problem with the church key/beer can situation came when men forgot to bring their church key with them. Imagine, you go fishing for the day and pack a cooler full of beer, but you leave the oh-so-important church key at home. You're screwed. Ermal Fraze (Ernie to his drinking buddies) can commiserate. In 1959, at a picnic, Ernie forgot his church key and tried in vain to open a can. He tried a car bumper, his teeth, and a tree branch but was unsuccessful. There had to be a better way, and Ernie was determined to find it. He set about to figure out how to build a better beer can. Insomnia would soon come to the rescue.

A few months later, when he couldn't sleep, Ernie found success. He first attempted to use a lever to poke a hole in the can, but the opening was sharp, so it was a no go. Then, he attached a pull ring to a small tab by the means of a heavy-duty rivet, and the pull-ring top was born. He sold his invention to the Aluminum Company of America, or Alcoa, for a nice tidy sum. Eventually, the Pittsburgh Beer Company put the pull rings on Iron City Beer and watched the sales take off. Within a few years virtually every beer and soda maker was using the pull-ring style of pop-top for their cans. The next innovative leap in the pop-top was due to the earliest days of the green movement.

MAN-DATE

In 1814, Francis Scott Key wrote the "Star Spangled Banner" as a poem. The music came from a British drinking song called the Anacreon.

People usually opened their cans and then tossed the pull rings off to the side. Environmentalists and anybody walking with bare feet hated the pull rings. Enter Dan Cudzik, a thirsty engineer working for the Reynolds Metals Company. He designed the toilet-bowl-shaped stay-on tab in 1975 that is still in use today. It was safe to walk barefoot at the beach again. And, as an added bonus, people were getting a great drink and helping make the world a little cleaner.

Today, if you're drinking canned beer and don't have a bottle opener, you're in the clear, but beer bottles still present a problem. Teeth have been known to open a few, along with car bumpers, key rings, butane lighters, and belt buckles. But the hands down I'm-a-guy-and-I-really-need-a-beer way to open a bottle is to use another bottle as a makeshift bottle opener. Take two beer bottles and invert one, place the caps where they overlap, and rapidly pull down on the lower bottle. Not only will you open one bottle, you often open two. Twice the love! Memo to idiots—or to those who have had too many beers—turn the top bottle of beer right-side-up quickly. You don't want to commit a party foul.

COLD-ACTIVATED BEER BOTTLES

Cold-activated beer bottles are a guy's best friend—and a great manvention. Men used to have to just wonder when the beer was cold, but now we can gaze lovingly at a Coors Light bottle and wait for the mountains to turn a nice wonderful shade of blue once the beer is cold. Coors is the leader in the cold-activated can market, but this manvention is too good to keep to themselves. We demand cold beer in all flavors! That is, unless you are European and are okay with your beer at room temperature, but most of us like it cold—and the colder the better.

The cold-activated bottles and cans use a thermochromic ink in the packaging. *Thermo* means heat and *chromic* means color. So thermochronic ink changes color when the temperature changes. The mountains on Coors Light labels begin to turn blue at 48°F and are fully blue at 44°F. Cans incorporate the same ink into the silk-screened label.

MAN-TASTIC FACT

Thermochromic ink is also found in the Pilot FriXion pen. The pen writes with normal looking ink, but it disappears with heat. The pen has a hard rubber knob where a pencil eraser would be. Rubbing the knob on your paper creates heat and "erases" the writing. You can magically bring it back by tossing it in the freezer for about ten minutes. Buy one and try it. It is a great party trick while you're waiting for the mountains to turn blue.

Cold-activated cans and bottles are a great manvention, but what we really need is thermoreactive beer. We need a genius to develop beer that instantly cools down when exposed to air. So if you're a genius, get to it! The men of the world are waiting.

THE KFC DOUBLE DOWN

Men like man food. We'll eat anything fried, sauced, and full of meat. And the KFC Double Down is the manliest meal on the planet. No bread, no lettuce, no tomatoes, it's nothing but meat. Instead of bread, you start with two chicken breasts (and what guy doesn't love breasts of any kind). Then, sandwiched between the two breasts, are two slices of cheese, one of pepper jack and one of Monterey. Also lurking in the middle of this meatheap are two slices of greasy, crispy bacon. Bacon makes the world go round (and often leads to heart attacks, but it is worth it). At the center of the Double Down, you'll find the Colonel's special

> ***MAN-TASTIC FACT***
>
> The Thousand Islands are actually real islands in the St. Lawrence River, straddling the United States–Canadian border northeast of Lake Ontario between Ontario, Canada, and New York state. The dressing got its name from the fact that all of the pickle pieces floating in the mayo-ketchup sauce looked just like the Thousand Islands.

sauce, which in reality is only Thousand Island dressing. So we have meat sandwiched around more meat, cheese, and a little special sauce. The best part is that if you read KFC's official nutrition info, the damn thing is actually better for you than a Big Mac. Two words: Man. Heaven.

JACK DANIELS

Men like their alcohol. Sometimes we are in the mood for light fare like beer, and sometimes we just need to go for the hard stuff. And hard man stuff is led by whiskey—or whisky if you prefer. *Whiskey* and *whisky* are both correct spellings. American and Irish distilleries tend to use the *e*. Scots, Canadians, Asians, and New Zealanders tend to spell it without the *e*. For proof that whiskey is an important man-vention, look no further than the word *whiskey*. Whiskey is derived from the Gaelic word *uisge*, a shortened version of *uisge beatha*, which means "water of life." That is proof enough for me!

MAN-TASTIC FACT

The word *scot* is an old English term meaning "reckoning." The English levied a scot as a tax, primarily on the entertainment industry. If you had a drink inside most cities, you would pay your scot as part of the drink price. Taverns would open up just outside of the city limits where you could go drink "scot-free."

MAN-DATE

When the United States gained control of Alaska in 1876, a ban on the sale of alcohol to native Alaskans was enacted. The natives learned how to make their own using sugar, flour, and fruit. The Alaskans called the liquor *hoochino*. After the Klondike gold rush of the late 1890s, the term was shortened to *hooch*, spread to the rest of the United States, and is still used today to describe homemade booze.

The secret to distilling whiskey came to the English isles between 1110 and 1300. Since the English isles didn't have many grapes, they distilled barley beer into what eventually became whiskey. Almost all whiskey was originally brewed in monasteries, further proof that God wanted us to have an occasional drink (who are we to argue with men of the cloth). All the early whiskey was used for medicine; it was either taken internally or externally as an antibiotic. Sure enough, whiskey is good for what ails you.

During those dark days of Prohibition, the U.S. government banned the manufacture of almost all alcohol. At first, medical alcohol (like whiskey) was still allowed. The pharmacy chain of Walgreens went from twenty to over 400 stores during Prohibition. Coincidence? Also, the actual act of drinking whiskey was never outlawed, so many people stocked up before the law went into effect. They found out the whiskey tasted better the longer it aged. Aged whiskeys are now among the most expensive drinks in the world. Also, it was more profitable to smuggle stronger whiskey, so many men developed a taste for the harder stuff.

Today, there are a bunch of distilleries that produce whiskey, and each produces a different type. Whiskey aficionados tend to usually have just one favorite brand that they stick to. Men tend to stay very loyal to a brand—until we get hammered, then it doesn't matter anymore. Many of the world's most famous breweries make malt whiskey, bourbon, or scotch. The only difference between these whiskeys is what they are made of and/or where they are made. Malt whiskeys, like Jameson and Bushmill, are made from at least 51% malted barley but can be made anywhere. Scotch whiskey (just called "scotch" by most of us) is also made from at least 51% malted barley and is distilled in . . . wait for it . . . Scotland, but in Scotland they just call it whisky. Famous scotches are Royal Crown, Johnnie Walker, and Dewar's.

> ### *MAN-TASTIC FACT*
>
> **White Lightning is named for its clear color. White Lightning is bottled right out of the still. Commercial whiskeys are aged in wooden casks. The wood helps give it the flavor and the color.**

Bourbon is made from at least 51% corn and is almost exclusively made in America. Famous bourbon brands are Maker's Mark and Wild Turkey. Tennessee whiskey is a special subset of bourbon whiskey that is filtered through charcoal. The leading producer of bourbon is Jack Daniels—a favorite manvention. Men love a good Jack and Coke, and Jack makes us feel great about buying American.

So, whether you spell it whiskey or whisky, the brown liquid is smooth going down, but drink too much and it won't be smooth coming back up. The food pyramid says grains are good for the body. So we can add nutritionists to God and doctors. Next time you hoist a glass, just remember you are doing it for religious, nutritional, and health reasons.

KINGSFORD CHARCOAL, LIGHTER FLUID, AND GIANT FLAMES

You may think that men don't like to cook, but all that changes when you add an open flame. What can we say, we like getting in touch with our inner caveman. And what better way to start an open flame than with two of the best manventions of all time: charcoal and lighter fluid. We squirt the lighter fluid onto the charcoal, launch a lit match in a graceful arc, and stand back as the fluid ignites with a six-foot-high whoosh. What's not to love?

Charcoal is just a carbon source (usually wood) that has been cooked in the absence of oxygen. This drives off the water and other volatile gases. What you are left with is a slow-burning fuel that doesn't create much smoke. Charcoal has been around for thousands of years as a source for cooking and for industrial energy. Many factories, blacksmith shops, and the like used charcoal as the primary energy source.

Charcoal was then brought into the cooking arena. It was great for indoor kitchens since the smoke was minimized. The funny thing is that smoke is actually desired because it adds to the flavor of the meat (or grilled tofu for you vegetarians). Barbeque snobs actually use wood chips on top of their charcoal to add a smoke flavor, and some barbeque snobs eschew charcoal all together in favor of cooking over wood. Wood may give a better taste, but the familiar charcoal briquette (a relatively new manvention) wins for ease of use. And as much as men love grilling, the majority of us still want to keep it simple.

The rounded brick briquette was actually invented by none other than Henry Ford, he of the Model T fame. Model Ts were made of wood rails combined with a metal frame and numerous other wood parts. Ford used the wood scraps left over from his car production to mass-produce charcoal briquettes. He eventually gave the production over to a relative named E. G. Kingsford, and the Kingsford Company was born. Men everywhere rejoiced!

MAN-TASTIC FACT

In the 1920s, a corner of almost all Ford dealer showrooms was set up to sell cooking supplies for the Ford Charcoal Company. Eventually the name was changed when Henry Ford shifted the company to a relative. It then became the Kingsford Company.

Today's briquettes contain mostly traditional charcoal and a few smaller ingredients. BBQ snobs will tell you the best briquettes come from hardwoods like maple, ash, and hickory, but a small amount of regular coal is usually added to keep the burning more even. An ash-whitening agent (such as lime) is added to give us a clue that it is time to put the meat on. Also, today's briquettes contain some type of nitrate to help them light. But lighter fluid is way more fun.

Yes, some barbequers start their grills with an electric charcoal starter. Boring! What is the fun in that? Lighter fluid lets men take our own lives in our hands. Yes, lighting the corner of a briquette may work just fine, but where is the danger in that? Some men just have to risk their eyebrows and knuckle hair in search of the perfect flame. A simple squirt of lighter fluid will do the trick, but men like to go big or go home (or to the hospital, depending). We usually empty half of the bottle, let it soak in for a minute, and flick the match. We are guaranteed to get either a great meal or an unintended rocket launch.

But what is lighter fluid? It is basically just a mixture of petroleum by-products that ignite very easily. After you squirt, allow the fluid to soak in for a minute before you light it. This allows many of the fumes to disappear, which results in better-tasting food. Another common grill lighter fuel is denatured alcohol (also called methylated spirits). Denatured means it has been rendered undrinkable. Since you can't create martinis with it, it is not subject to a sin tax and is cheaper. Whatever fluid you use, remember to let the coals get white-hot before you grill your meat.

Charcoal and lighter fluid have been a favorite backyard man-vention for nearly a century. Throw in a fancy grill and a set of Titanium barbeque tools and we'll stay outside grilling until the cows come home—as a medium-rare steak fillet, that is.

CHIMNEY STARTERS, BBQ TONGS, AND TELESCOPING FORKS

Some men opt to keep their knuckle hair when grilling—which is fine. After all, what good is a perfectly seasoned rack of ribs if you're not around to eat it. For knuckle-hair-loving men and guys who just love gadgets, there are tongs and extending forks. And for men who don't love the smell of burnt lighter fluid (there are a few), there are chimney starters. Let's start with starters (pun intended).

Chimney starters look like a chimney (shocking, I know), and you fill them up with charcoal. Then you stuff balled up paper underneath the chimney and light the paper on fire. The flame lights the bottom briquettes and then walks up the chimney and lights the entire column. You avoid toxic fumes from the burnt lighter fluid *and* you get

MAN-TASTIC FACT

The word *buccaneer* comes from *boucanier*, which means "to smoke meat on a boucan (barbeque)." Since marauding pirates of the West Indies cooked meat (usually wild boar or manatee) over an open flame, the name stuck.

to keep your eyebrows; it's definitely the choice for safety-conscious men. You can even cook directly over the chimney starter if you are trying to flash sear a steak or fish.

Telescoping forks and barbeque tongs also make men feel like men—without risking life or limb. Barbeque tongs let you grab your meat from up to eighteen inches away, safe from the flame in most cases, but if you need to poke your meat from a greater distance, telescoping forks are the way to go, and they make you look cool while you do it. A good set of tools will set you back a few dollars, but think of it as an investment. Better tools equal fewer hospital bills. And, of course, wielding a good set of barbeque tools will also make you look like a Klingon in battle. What could be better?

GAS GRILLS

As we've discussed, men have been burning meat over open flame since the dawn of man, but sometimes we just don't want to wait for the charcoal or wood chips to heat up. Again, men are impatient—especially when food is involved. Enter the gas grill, the most convenient way to burn meat. The switch from burning wood to burning natural gas (or propane) was one of convenience. Wood fires were replaced by charcoal in the 1930s because charcoal was easier to transport and light. Today, hardcore meat burners still swear by charcoal for flavor, but many of us opt for the convenience of gas grills. Interestingly enough, this manvention actually started out as a marketing gimmick.

The decade that brought us hippies, psychedelic drugs, and mini-skirts also blessed men everywhere with the gas grill. William Wepfer and Melton Lancaster, who both worked for the Arkansas Louisiana Gas Company, were looking for new ways to market natural gas and created the first gas grills. They basically converted an egg-shaped charcoal grill to run off gas, but gas grills sure have changed since the 1960s.

Today, gas grills are the kings of man ease. We still get the potential catastrophe of losing our eyebrows (albeit a smaller chance), but we get instant heat to cook with. Gas grills also give you a range of options. You can have from two up to twenty burners. You can have infrared heating elements if you want.

MAN-TASTIC FACT

While many of us use the terms *grill* and *barbeque* interchangeably, there is a difference to purists. Grilling is fast cooking over an open flame. Barbeque is indirect slow cooking over a low, smoky fire.

You can have grills made out of materials ranging from good old steel all the way to porcelain. You can get really exotic tools made out of titanium or aircraft aluminum. You can get fancy smoker boxes to mimic the smokiness of charcoal. The sky is the limit, and the gas grill gives men a reason to shop.

I can hear you now, *but men don't shop*! Well, men may not be fans of shopping until it comes time to look for a new grill and accessories. When that wonderful day happens, buckle up for an all-day excursion to any store that sells tools and gas grills. Every spring you can find glossy-eyed men wandering the gas grill aisle looking for the latest in man appliances. Gas grills are a man's best friend—until we run out of gas. But even then we see the bright side; an empty tank of gas is just another reason to head out and look for grill accessories.

BEER (NEED I SAY MORE?)

Beer has been called the elixir of the gods, liquid gold, and even liquid bread. But whatever you call it, beer is a damn fine manvention. So let's take a moment to celebrate its illustrious history.

Beer is as old as any liquid this side of water; historians speculate that man actually learned how to create beer before he baked bread. The first beer was probably brewed by accident about 9,000 years ago. If exposed to water and air, any grain will naturally break down and start to ferment. Some lucky ancient likely picked up the pulpy mess and drank the liquid that he squeezed out of it and beer was born. The oldest recorded records of beer were from the Sumerians about 6,000 years ago. Sumer was situated between the Tigris and Euphrates Rivers, which many people believe is also the location of the Garden of Eden. This is enough proof to me that it is the elixir of the gods. Even the noted American Ben Franklin said, "Beer is proof that God loves us and wants us to be happy." And who are we to question Ben Franklin.

MAN-TASTIC FACT

The *Mayflower* sailed from England with a belly full of beer, and it landed at Plymouth Rock because the beer was running low (and the seas were rough). The Pilgrims were actually headed for the mouth of the Hudson River (New York City today).

Some experts also say that society went from being hunter-gatherers to farmers so men could grow enough grain for beer. And beer has been present in almost every civilization since then. Asia, South America, and Africa all had forms of beer using locally grown grain, but there were a few societies that tilted their nose at this delicious manvention. Notably, the Greeks and Romans considered beer a low-class beverage since they were so into wine. No wonder their civilizations disappeared.

In the last half of the Middle Ages, beer brewing shifted from a family tradition to larger-scale production. It was primarily brewed in monasteries and convents, which is even more proof of beer being heaven sent. Large-scale beer brewing as we know it began to appear all over Europe, and it soon spread to the United States.

In the mid-1700s, the Industrial Revolution helped beer breweries proliferate around the world. The steam engine, thermometers, and refrigeration led to beer aplenty. Also, the migration from rural settings to urban centers allowed for the corner pubs to become a staple in life. In the United States, beer brewing took on a serious bent in a town named after the Algonquin word for gathering place, Milwaukee.

Milwaukee became the beer capital of North America in the mid-1800s for several reasons. First, a large German immigrant population brought their home-brew recipes with them. Names like Schlitz, Miller, and Pabst are just a few of the better-known ones. Second, close access to a large lumber trade made it easy to get wooden kegs made. Stainless steel kegs didn't show up until one hundred years later. Third, Milwaukee was a medium-sized town but had lake access to ship cheaply to bigger cities, like Chicago, Cleveland, and Detroit. The battles between the beer companies in Milwaukee were ferocious.

> **MAN-TASTIC FACT**
>
> **A recipe for beer was actually found on the wall inside King Tut's tomb.**

Another milestone in American brewing occurred when Adolphus Busch married the daughter of Eberhard Anheuser in the mid-1800s. It was truly a match made in heaven, and a beer dynasty was born. This company set up in St. Louis, which had access to the Mississippi River. Busch also decided to brew cold and ship cold, which was a first. But it was a beer inspired by Budweis,

Germany, that helped them to the top. All hail Budweiser, King of Beers!

> **MAN-DATE**
>
> In 1876, Louis Pasteur applied his pasteurization process to beer to keep it from spoiling. That was twenty-two years before the same process was used on milk. It's funny the things your high school biology teachers never mentioned.

Surprisingly, the noble experiment of Prohibition in the 1920s helped streamline the American beer-making industry. How did Prohibition actually help the beer industry? Well, smaller beer breweries went out of business, and some breweries switched to bottling sodas and bottled water. Some started producing near beer, which still contained alcohol. Often the beer was watered down to help with profits, and women loved the low alcohol content of the new product. And if women drink beer, men are bound to follow. After Prohibition was repealed in 1933, these lighter alcohol beers continued to be sold in the United States, and as with any new product, advertising was soon to follow.

Beer ads have always been a part of male life. In the 1930s and 1940s, baseball was synonymous with beer ads, and baseball was America's game. Anheuser-Busch actually owned the St. Louis Cardinals from 1953 to 1996, and Coors Field and Busch Stadium are still in existence today. But the explosion of television ads promoted U.S. beer making to new heights. Frogs, Clydesdales, Spuds, Bud Bowls, Whassssup, real men of genius, and the "king of beers" all led Busch to a number one market share. Right behind is Miller, which introduced Lite beer with "great taste,

> ### *MAN-TASTIC FACT*
>
> **In English pubs, beer is sold in pints and quarts. The saying "mind your Ps and Qs" means to be on your best behavior and reportedly came from English bartenders.**

less filling." Of course, Miller also created Milwaukee's Best, a.k.a. the Beast, which is a cheap college favorite—and what guy doesn't like cheap beer?

In the past thirty years, home brewing and microbrewing have taken off. Home brewing started legally in the United States in 1978 after Congress repealed a Prohibition law still on the books that prevented it. It is legal to brew up to 100 gallons per adult in a household. Of course, you can't sell it, but you can definitely have the guys over. Many of these earlier home brewers liked it so much they started their own microbreweries. Microbrewers typically make less than 15,000 barrels of beer and are taxed at a lower rate than large-scale breweries. Microbrew brewmasters tend to be more inventive and craft specialty beers. If you want raspberry-flavored beer, they can make it. But the best part about specialty beers is that brewers can pick crazy names like Santa's Butt, Alimony Ale, and my favorite, Goat Scrotum Ale. Microbreweries now amount to almost 10 percent of the U.S. suds market.

But no matter what brand you drink or what kind you like, beer is here to stay. So raise your drinking glass to one of mankind's greatest manventions!

BEER HELMETS

If you are a man and you drink beer—and chances are you do—one accessory is a much-needed manvention: the beer helmet. You are guaranteed to be the hit of the frat party or any NASCAR race. Pop on that plastic hat, slide in a couple of bottles, and you have hands-free beer.

Men love beer helmets mainly because they leave our hands free. They're like a frat party Snuggie. We can play beer pong (another great manvention), pay for pizza, and get our groove on out on the dance floor. Now a man can get his swerve on and still enjoy a little adult beverage.

NASCAR races are another locale ideally suited for the beer helmet. You have two hands free to cheer, a hat to protect you from the sun, and, well, beer. This could be the best manvention ever for NASCAR fans. Even the nondrinkers can slide in a couple of bottles of aqua, so the beer helmet is perfect for men of all ages.

The inventor of the beer helmet is lost to history, and that is a shame. Here is a man (frat boy?) who truly deserves to be revered. But for at least thirty years we have worshipped his wonderful manvention.

MR. COFFEE AND THE KEURIG

Ah coffee! That wonderful brown liquid that we use to either crank us up or sometimes to help us sober up. Just imagine a world without coffee: We'd stumble into the shower to try to wake up, but it would only momentarily revive us from the death of sleep. We'd damn near wreck our cars as we drove in a sleep-driven fog. We'd stumble into work and take two hours to get productive. But worst of all, we wouldn't be able to take a coffee break! Our bosses would expect us to work eight hours straight. Coffee is pretty amazing, but coffee beans would be useless without the beloved modern manvention of the coffee pot.

> ***MAN-TASTIC FACT***
>
> Hawaii is the only state in the United States in which coffee is grown commercially. Coffee is the second-largest import in the world (after oil).

Coffee has been around ever since a goat herder in Ethiopia

first noticed the strange behavior of his goats after eating coffee beans. Seeing that his goats acted more energized after eating the berries from a particular bush, the goat herder sampled them himself and experienced the same effect. The coffee beans tasted like hell, but the goat herder shared the beans with some monks who roasted some of the berries and noticed that the berries sure smell good when burnt. The burnt remains dissolved in water led to the first cup of joe. But we owe our daily cup of mud to a displaced American.

Sir Benjamin Thompson was an American ex-pat who invented the percolating coffee pot. He was also a noted scientist in the area of thermodynamics, so his scientific pursuits and coffee experimentation were a perfect combination. Being a loyalist, inventor, and scientist earned him the titles of Sir and Count Rumford, but it took another mister to change coffee permanently in the 1970s. His name? Mr. Coffee.

The Mr. Coffee coffeemaker was the first coffeemaker that allowed consumers to drip-brew their own coffee at home. Drip brewing (hot water dripping through grounds and a paper filter) is by far the most popular form of coffee brewing in the West now. Mr. Coffee coffeemakers were a staple in the 1970s and 1980s, and the technology is still alive and in use in most offices and kitchens today. Mr. Coffee made coffee so easy to make that even us men could do it by ourselves.

> **MAN-TASTIC FACT**
>
> Coffee beans are actually a berry.

When we give the award to the lazy man's coffeemaker, the hands-down winner is the Keurig. First of all, the space-age Keurig looks really cool on the counter; it's sleek, black, and manly, which we love. Second, the Keurig wins on convenience. Grab the handle at the top and open it up (just like lifting a toilet seat). Drop in a K-Cup of your favorite adrenalin-boosting caffeine and close the top. The machine does the rest, and sixty seconds later you are sipping a cup of black gold. No mess, no fuss, and a perfectly made caffeinated beverage. The Keurig truly is the perfect manvention.

MAN-DATE

A Mr. Coffee coffeemaker appeared in the movie *Apollo 13*. This would have been wonderful except the Apollo 13 tragedy happened in 1970 and the Mr. Coffee was introduced in 1972.

Every day, millions of men worship at the altar of the coffee pot. From its insides pours the juice of life: instant energy in a cup. For cubicle dwellers, the coffee pot gives you an excuse to leave your desk and wander the building. For drivers on your way into work, it gives you an excuse to flirt with that cute barista at the corner store. And for the late-night revelers, it gives you a way to wake up for the cab ride home. I guess you could just call any guy Mr. Coffee.

TOP TEN BEST MANVENTIONS FROM THE 1970S

1. The van
2. Shag carpet
3. Pet Rocks
4. Disco
5. Pong
6. Disco balls
7. Leisure suits
8. *Star Wars*
9. Sea-Monkeys
10. Silly String

CHAPTER 4

OUT AND ABOUT:

MEN ON THE MOVE

INSIDE THIS CHAPTER YOU WILL FIND:

- ☑ ATM MACHINES
- ☑ PAINTBALL GUNS
- ☑ PUBLIC URINALS AND URINAL CAKES
- ☑ SUPERMAN, WOODIES, AND OTHER THRILL RIDES
- ☑ STYROFOAM BEER COOLERS
- ☑ ZIPPO LIGHTERS, PISTOL GRIPS, AND FIRE LAMPS
- ☑ DRIVE-THROUGH RESTAURANTS AND FAST FOOD
- ☑ LEVI'S BLUE JEANS
- ☑ POCKETS AND CARGO PANTS
- ☑ BOXERS, BRIEFS, AND TIGHTY-WHITIES
- ☑ BUILT-IN STADIUM CUP HOLDERS
- ☑ VUVUZELAS
- ☑ THUNDERSTICKS

If men like anything it's having fun. And, while there are cool things to do at your house, sometimes you just need to go out, party, and have fun. And if you are going to go out on the town, you need stuff to do it with, like money, beer coolers, and more, depending on how you roll. You also need great destinations, cool clothes, and a place to piss when needed. So, put on your favorite pair of jeans as we examine all of the great manventions that help us get out and about.

ATM MACHINES

Back when I was in college, I learned that cash was king. (After all, you can't make it rain with plastic.) And when men go out on the town, we need quick access to cash. Fortunately, automated teller machines (ATMs) are a great manvention for men who work and men who party late.

Luther Simjian, a prodigious inventor, created the first ATM prototype in 1939. His "hole-in-the-wall-machine" allowed a person to do business without seeing a teller face to face. It was withdrawn from service after only six months because almost no one used it. Seems like the only people who wanted to bank without being face-to-face at the time were gamblers and prostitutes. It took a few more years for men to be able to grab cash on the fly.

In the mid-1960s, John Shepherd-Barron, the director of De La Rue Instruments, was relaxing in his tub when he got ticked because he couldn't get his own money from the bank on the weekend. He decided to solve the problem himself, and his first ATM machine opened in London in 1967. His machine was a little different because it didn't use plastic cards. The machine used single-use checks (okay, they were actually *cheques* since it was in London). In exchange for the cheques, which were impregnated with mildly radioactive carbon 14, and a PIN,

MAN-TASTIC FACT

John Shepherd-Barron invented the personal identification number (PIN), but he wanted a six-digit code. His wife said she could only remember four digits and won that argument.

the ATM would dispense cash. Barclays, one of London's most prominent banks, insisted that Shepherd-Barron not patent the device because if crooks could figure out how the machine decoded the cheque, they could rob the machines. However, despite the convenience, the entire concept of radioactive cheques was not a welcome idea for most men. Guys usually keep their wallets in their pockets, and pockets are real close to their nuts. Clearly, nuts and radioactivity are not a man-friendly mix. So, goodbye cheques. Hello keypad.

James Goodfellow of Scotland is purported to be the first to invent a machine that used a card and a keypad. The only problem was the machine kept the card as a record of the transaction. Although Mr. Goodfellow created a great idea, it was a few years before you could get your money and your card back. The Smithsonian's National Museum of American History recognizes American Don Wetzel as the inventor of the first networked ATM machine. And this machine gave you your card back! Finally, we had the ATM machine we are familiar with, and thank heaven for it. It's the only way to get quick cash in the middle of the night to

MAN-TASTIC FACT

Dimes and quarters have ridges on the edge to keep crooks at bay. In the olden days, these coins were made from silver and didn't have ridges. Scoundrels would shave silver from the edge and still use the smaller coin. The ridges were designed to show if a coin had been shaved. Pennies and nickels were made from cheap metals so this feature wasn't necessary.

pay bail bondsmen, bookies, strippers, barmaids, or if you just need a little grub. Thank you Don Wetzel for making men's lives just a little easier.

PAINTBALL GUNS

Paintball is a game made for men. Where else do you get to dress up like you're in the military, go to the woods, and then shoot your best friends? It's a great way to blow off some steam—and some carbon dioxide—and if you're lucky, you get some awesome bruises to brag about with your friends.

Paintball guns were first developed in the 1940s by the Nelson Paint Company to mark trees in hard-to-reach places. Farmers would also use them to mark cattle for sale, trade, or slaughter. In 1981, the first recorded incident of paintball, twelve buddies from New Hampshire played a version of capture the flag as they shot their friends with tree-marking pistols. The first paintball field opened a year later in Rochester, New York, and men have been hooked ever since.

Paintball guns have evolved over the years. The first guns were single-shot guns that had to be cocked each time to fire. Boring! New guns are actually computer driven and can fire up to thirty-two rounds a second. The gel-filled capsules are impressively launched with carbon dioxide from a compressed cartridge on the gun. If you've ever been hit with a paintball, you know paint balls leave a serious welt when they hit, which is why some players wear padded clothing. Man up guys! Those welts are just motivation to be better.

Paintball is one of the world's largest extreme sports now, and it even boasts several professional leagues around the world, including two in the United States. The games are usually total team elimination or a capture-the-flag type. Imagine telling your dad that you are dropping out of college to go pro in paintball. My dad might have used a real gun on my ass after that conversation. But whether you've gone pro or are just a weekend warrior, paintball guns are one testosterone-inducing manvention.

MAN-DATE

The first gun created specifically for playing paintball was the aptly named Splatmaster, which went on the market in 1985.

PUBLIC URINALS AND URINAL CAKES

When it comes to relieving ourselves, men have a distinct advantage. We are blessed with anatomy that lets us do most of our business from a distance. A quick zip, a little pee, a gentle shake, a hand washing, and we are gone. When we're out of the house, we sit if we have to, but only in emergencies. Most of the time, we use our next amazing manvention: the public urinal.

We can thank one unlucky Roman soldier for the idea of a urinal. While on the way home from a victorious battle, he spotted a trough complete with running water, which we all know hastens the urge to answer the call of nature. He let go with his flow only to find out that he had just pissed into the aquifer for the town. For his mistake, he was castrated and spent the rest of his life as a slave. Since then men have pissed in pots, troughs, and latrines, but the urinal that we know and love was patented by Andrew Rankin in the United States in 1866. To say that men everywhere were relieved is an understatement that you won't understand if you haven't peed into a trough (or an aquifer). But with urinals came urinal etiquette, and I feel confident that Emily Post doesn't have a chapter on pissing in public.

In order to use a urinal, men must follow a strict code of conduct. At the top of the list is the singlemost important urinal rule: You must leave an empty urinal between

> ***Man-tastic Fact***
>
> **The largest public restroom in the world is a four-story, 30,000-square-foot edifice with over 1,000 toilets located in China (hey, a billion people need to pee). It even has an outdoor area for men so they can pee under the stars. The restroom also contains whimsical urinals that look like crocodile mouths and Virgin Mary lookalikes (uh-oh, someone is going to Hell).**

you and your neighbor, if at all possible. As a matter of fact, urinal selection is critical. If the room is empty, choose an end urinal. If one other person is in the room, choose the urinal at the opposite end of the bathroom. If both ends are occupied, choose the one in the center. The next person in has to use a stall or risk the scorn of all other men in the room. However, in extremely crowded rooms, the empty-urinal rule is temporarily waived for the duration of your stay.

Restrooms almost always contain an odd number of urinals to help with the empty-urinal rule. Next time you go, count them up. If builders only have room for two urinals, they will put up a privacy barrier. Privacy barriers are a recent trend that allow the empty-urinal rule to be discarded.

Other urinal rules are also important to remember as well. Leave the junior varsity (JV) urinals for kids and short guys. JV urinals are generally placed at one end, so you may have to bend the empty-urinal rule in some cases. Remember, short guys already have it hard enough in life. At least leave them the pleasure of peeing downhill. In addition, never talk to anyone you don't know while you are doing your business; always look straight ahead at the wall. Sports bars often help by putting up the sports page over the urinal. Noise needs to be kept to minimum, but emitting an "aaaahhhhh" is allowed if you have been drinking beer. Talking to close friends is allowed if you end up in the room together, but it must be about sports, music, or women. Heart-to-heart dude talks need to be shared in a less intimate setting.

You also want to at least try to use good aim. Hitting the urinal is not that hard (when you're sober). Use your hand to steady it if you have an errant man-hose. If you find that you're having trouble, aim at the urinal cake. The familiar cakes (also called urinal mints, toilet cakes, toilet sweet tarts, bathroom breath mints, trough lollies, piss biscuits, and so on) that litter the bottom of our urinals are a great manvention. We get a clean urinal and a target to pee at—and research has shown that men do better with a target.

The familiar mints are usually pink, but they can come in any color or shape, and many now come with pictures. The base of the cake is usually composed of naphthalene, which is the main ingredient in mothballs. It must work because I have never seen moths in a restroom. The cakes are also infused with sweet-smelling compounds to mask other offensive smells. They also kill germs and help keep the urinal clean. Many are sold with a cute plastic spider web to keep the mint in place.

Some companies have jumped on the advertising bandwagon and

MAN-TASTIC FACT

Ernest Hemingway loved bars, drinking, and cats. He combined his interests and converted a urinal from his favorite bar (Sloppy Joe's in Key West) into a drinking fountain for his beloved multifingered cats. Let's all hope Papa never got confused and used it for its previous purpose.

are using the cakes to make a profit. The cakes can be molded into any shape and made of any color, so they're great advertising tools. In addition, Healthquest Technologies now sells the Wizmark (a perfect name for this device), an interactive urinal communicator. This handy device is a urinal mint and plastic screen with flashing lights and a voice-recorded message for those guys with great aim. Some tell you not to drink and drive, but some have been placed in bars to advertise new types of beer. A few have been more creative, and Country Music Television used them to advertise their Bad Boys of Country specials. Just like real estate, advertising is all about location, location, location.

So fortunately for guys, gone are the days of peeing in a trough. With privacy barriers and talking urinal cakes, pissing has now become a deluxe experience—thanks to these wonderful manventions.

SUPERMAN, WOODIES, AND OTHER THRILL RIDES

Men love the thrill of pushing the envelope, especially if it's done in a safe, controlled environment. Roller coasters fit the bill. They scare the crap out of us but are perfectly safe—the perfect manvention.

Roller coasters date back to the Russian ice slides that were popular in the 1700s. Ice slides were tall slides in which you rode a wooden sled to the bottom. But they had one design flaw: no ice equals no ride. Nobody is sure who first decided to put wheels on the sled, but one thing that is not debated is the actual first "coaster" in the United States. The Mauch Chunk railway in Pennsylvania was designed to haul coal up an incredibly steep hill with mules during the day. But at night the men took over the train to have their own fun. They would haul a car loaded with people up to the top and then let them go, and the roller coaster was born. Even after the trains weren't needed to move the coal, they still operated as a roller coaster for a dollar a ride. Only a man would think to turn a coal train track into a gold mine and forever change the way we have fun.

> **MAN-TASTIC FACT**
>
> None of the stores in the Disney parks sell gum. That means less gum to get stuck under the rides or on the shoes of those looking for a magical experience.

Soon men were building roller coasters all over the eastern seaboard, but Coney Island was king. Between the Civil War and World War II, the area was roller coaster heaven. Men went there to be scared and to ride on the wooden roller coasters, or "woodies." Of course, back then, all the roller coasters were woodies

and hard-core coaster fans (purists) still love getting wood, but steel is the way to go for ultimate acrobatic thrills. And we owe steel coasters to the inventor of the most famous rodent ever.

> **MAN-TASTIC FACT**
>
> The Beast at King's Island in Ohio is the longest "woodie" in the world at well over a mile long.

Walt Disney (he of the rat fame) opened the first steel tube roller coaster at Disneyland in 1959 and changed coasting forever. Steel frames allow coasters to flip, loop, and corkscrew. Since then, men have continually upped the adrenalin factor of roller coasters. Higher, faster, and more death-defying is what men want, and the theme-park industry is glad to oblige.

Today, there is a new design feature that is creeping into roller coasters. Traditional roller coasters start by slowly winching you up a giant drop hill; the higher the hill, the faster the drop. But new roller coaster design turns the entire car (including you) into a giant bullet to be launched. Superman: The Escape (at a Six Flags Magic Mountain near you) is a great example of this type of coaster. When you ride Superman, the coaster starts on the ground and uses linear induction motors to launch you. You get launched over an L-shaped track that extends a football field into the air, and you get some serious hang time at the top before you hurtle backwards back to the starting gate. Linear induction motors give steel coasters a greater rate of acceleration, and anything that helps men move faster is okay in our book. So bring on the controlled mayhem and a great coaster; we're more than willing to go along for the ride.

STYROFOAM BEER COOLERS

Men try to be green. We carry reusable water bottles with us when we go for a hike. We recycle all of the plastic bottles and beer cans that make it into our house. We care about the environment. But there is one manvention that we love enough to say screw the environment: Styrofoam beer coolers.

Professional drunks usually have a plastic cooler in their car for beer runs, but since most men do not plan ahead, we often buy Styrofoam beer coolers to save the day. You're heading to the lake with friends and need to grab some brews and ice? A quick trip into your local Stop-n-Rob convenience store will set you up with all you need. Most coolers are designed for a one-way trip. We consume the beer, the ice melts, and the cooler is broken when a fat guy tries to sit on it. Then we toss the pieces into a nearby trash can. It is estimated that only one out of every seventy-five Styrofoam beer coolers are reused. Yes, they're not good for the environment, but they're still a pretty kick-ass manvention.

MAN-DATE

Styrofoam coolers are a hit with the medical industry too. They are used to transport hearts, lungs, kidneys, blood, and so on.

ZIPPO LIGHTERS, PISTOL GRIPS, AND FIRE LAMPS

Fire has always amazed men, and with the advent of lighters, man could control that flame and easily carry it with him. In the early days, man needed one flame to start another. A German chemist changed all that with the manvention that paved the way to portable fire: the lighter.

In 1832, Johann Dobereiner invented a clunky fire lamp, which used sulfuric acid (battery acid to you and me) and zinc to create hydrogen gas. He sprayed hydrogen gas onto platinum powder (which was kind of expensive) and heat was created. And where there's heat, you'll also find man's greatest love: fire. But the fire lamp gave rise to the need for a more portable, safer, and less expensive version. Flint scraping against steel had been used for many years to create sparks, which can ignite anything flammable, but it was temperamental. Along came ferrocerium to save the day. Ferrocerium was a man-made alloy that generates much hotter sparks when scraped with metal. Many lighters still use a ferrocerium wheel to generate a spark, but some use a piezoelectric crystal that creates an electric spark when compressed. They are commonly used as electronic igniters in gas grills and lighters.

> **MAN-TASTIC FACT**
>
> Since WWII, every U.S. Navy warship has had its own Zippo lighter. The lighter features the name, number, and a picture of the ship engraved onto the side of the lighter case.

Naptha (still used in lighter fluid) was one of the first fuels of choice because it burned easy, but it stunk real bad. The switch from naptha to butane in the 1950s led to today's lighters. Butane is a liquid under pressure and if you allow the liquid to expand it becomes a vapor and vapors light easier. Butane also didn't smell as bad as naptha. Butane is the fuel for almost all lighters nowadays.

Today, lighters can run the gamut from cheap disposables all the way to fancy pistol-grip torches. Two of the best lighters on the market are made by the Ronson and Zippo companies, which both started making lighters in the early 1900s. Their lighters were and are portable and reliable—and let's be honest, Zippos are pretty awesome. So fire up a lighter and get in touch with your inner caveman.

DRIVE-THROUGH RESTAURANTS AND FAST FOOD

Men love convenience, which makes drive-through restaurants a favorite manvention. But compared to some of our favorite things, drive-thrus are relatively new and uniquely American. Just make sure you have a car, since most drive-thrus won't serve pedestrians or bicycle riders.

Drive-thrus are different than drive-ins. Drive-ins had been around for a while when drive-thrus were created. For those of us under fifty, a drive-in involves pulling into a parking spot and being served in your car by a roller-skating carhop, who may or may not accidentally spill food in your lap. A few new chains, like Sonic, have re-emerged to cater to this nostalgia.

Drive-ins started to disappear as cars shrunk. A 1950s American car had a front seat bigger than my living room. Eating in your car wasn't difficult—neither was making love, but that is another story. As cars shrunk, taking a date to a drive-in was never as much fun. Maybe Sonic (and the like) has re-emerged because cars and SUVs have grown in size.

The first actual drive-thru restaurant opened in California in 1948. Harry and Esther Snyder's business plan was to give people food, fast and cheap. The original In-N-Out Burgers were only drive-thrus, since they had no indoor seating area. In-N-Out restaurants were so popular that many are still in business today, mostly in California.

McDonald's first opened a drive-thru for a very practical (and moneymaking) reason. In 1975, A McDonald's franchise owner in Sierra Vista, Arizona, catered to a U.S. Army rule to explode

MAN-DATE

In 1952, Glen Bell started a hamburger and hot dog stand in the sleepy town of San Bernardino, which just happened to be the same place that the McDonald brothers were starting up. Bell adroitly switched to Mexican food and opened Taco Tia. It wasn't until 1962 that Glen opened the first Taco Bell.

the drive-thru business. Seems the servicemen at nearby Fort Huachuca weren't allowed to exit a car if they were wearing their uniforms off base. The intrepid franchisee saw all of those hungry GIs driving by and decided to give them an option. The drive-thru at Mickey Ds was born. Over half of McDonald's sales today come through the window at the drive-thru.

Today, you can get almost any type of food—burgers, chicken, coffee, donuts, you name it—from a drive-thru. The convenience and cost of fast food has made drive-thrus a way of life in the United States, but they have been slower to catch on overseas. But I feel this manvention will someday achieve world domination.

MAN-DATE

In 1996, McDonald's opened a McSki ski-through window in Salen, Sweden.

LEVI'S BLUE JEANS

Blue jeans are the quintessential guy wear. They're comfortable, tough, and you really can't tell if they're dirty. In fact, most men would have had to go through high school and college naked if not for this manvention.

The claim for the origin of these beloved pants is debated among scholars. One camp traces its roots back to the French, who produced a fabric called "serge de Nimes" (twill from Nimes). But serge de Nimes was actually a silk and wool blend, so that may be a stretch. The term *jeans* is thought to come from a type of pants worn by the sailors from Genoa. These blue pants were durable and great for hard work.

Regardless of the origin of the fabric, it took two icons to make them popular. The first was Loeb Strauss, a German immigrant who chased the money from New York to the gold rush of California. He opened a dry goods store and supplied whatever was needed to small shops and gold prospectors. Along the way, he changed his name to Levi Strauss and—with a little help from a tailor—became an icon. In 1872, a Reno tailor named Jacob Davis suggested that he and Levi add copper rivets to the stress points to make the work pants more durable. The familiar riveted jean was born the next year.

Why are jeans blue? Well, jeans made great work pants and were called "waist overalls." Work pants are going to get dirty, and since most of the cotton, linen, and wool fibers that make up the denim are light in color, the makers needed to add some color to hide the stains. Indigo dye was the cheapest dark dye available, so blue jeans were born. How would the world have changed if a cheap mustard yellow dye had been the only one available? Today, the jeans we know and love are dark and durable, and, as any college student knows, they

MAN-TASTIC FACT

Why do we call it a "pair of pants"? The word *pants* is short for *pantaloons*. Pantaloon was the name of an idiot in an Italian comedy. He was always dressed in trousers, and his name was eventually adopted for clothes. In the early days, leg coverings were actually two pieces that tied together at the top, so a pair makes sense.

can go several days (or weeks) without washing. (I'm not proud of the fact now, but two pairs of jeans could last me an entire four-week wash cycle in college.) But jeans were still primarily work wear until after World War II.

The influence of movies and music caused the jean to take its rightful place as the king of guy wear. The second cultural icon stepped up to the plate next. When James Dean epitomized cool with his blue jeans and attitude, guys flocked to imitate the look. Around the same time, Levi's went nationwide and Levi's jeans became the number one brand. Many other companies have since been added to the mix, but regardless of who makes them, jeans are king for men from all walks of life, and we also love them for how they look on women.

In the 1970s, designer jeans took off with the female set, and men stood up and paid attention. What guy doesn't like the look of

MAN-TASTIC FACT

Levi's jeans are stitched with orange thread to match the color of the copper rivets. During WWII, the familiar orange Levi's seagull flying across your ass pocket look was temporarily halted to save thread for the war effort.

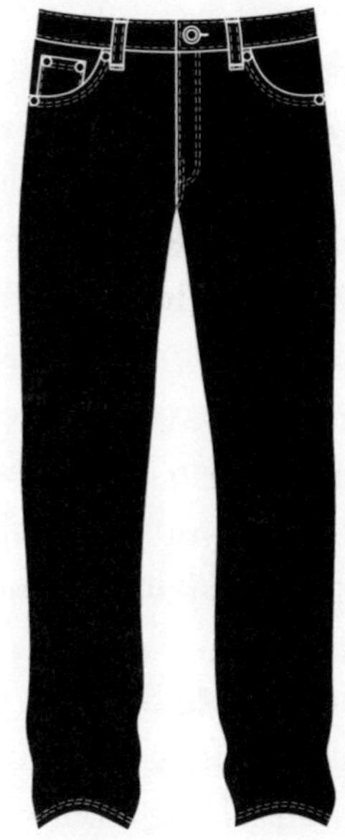

the female form in a nice tight pair of jeans? The tighter the better. Since the designer days, jeans have been stone washed, acid washed, ripped on purpose, changed colors, and have gotten more expensive, but we still love them.

Blue jeans definitely deserve their place on the manvention list. Even if our jobs require us to wear nicer pants, we still long for the carefree days when we could just throw on a pair of jeans as we ran out the door—which is what we still do, when we can get away with it.

POCKETS AND CARGO PANTS

Have you ever seen all the crap that women carry around in their purses? Well, men have stuff, too. No, we don't have nearly as much as our better halves, but we still have to carry around our keys, wallet, cash, coins, and cell phones. And if we're going to have stuff, we need a place to store it. Most men, with the exception of urban metrosexuals or NBA players, wouldn't even think of carrying a purse—and no, changing the name to "man bag" doesn't make it okay. Instead, us guys need pockets to store our stuff. And if we are going to have pockets, why not take it over the top. Enter our next manvention: the cargo pant.

In jolly old England, pockets were simply a pouch used to put coins in (purple velvet Crown Royal bags anyone?). These pockets would hang from our belt but weren't safe from nefarious pickpockets. So men stuffed their dangling pockets inside their trousers. But stuffing the pocket inside the pants was uncomfortable—it could irritate the other things that were hanging around your trousers—and also inconvenient to get at. To solve the problem, a daring man cut a slit in his trousers and the modern pocket soon followed. Patch pockets (a.k.a. hip pockets) were soon sewn onto the back for carrying the old wallet. Most pants also have slash pockets on the front, which makes things a lot easier than carrying around some old pouch, and for that we are forever grateful.

MAN-TASTIC FACT

The pocket mouse has a fur-lined external cheek pouch that opens next to his mouth. He uses the pouch to store seeds and nuts when he is making a grocery run. Every man needs a safe place for his nuts.

If those four basic pockets won't do, you can always go with cargo pants, which are often stocked with more flaps than the law allows. Cargo pants initially showed up in the uniform world (think SWAT teams and Army Rangers) but crossed over into the mainstream because we men like places for our stuff. Cargo pants were initially worn by the rugged outdoor types, and high-end cargo pants even have zip-off legs for the true outdoorsman. If it gets too damn hot, just zip off the legs. If it gets chilly, just zip them back on. But even if we seldom leave our air-conditioned man caves, we want to be able to when ready. Think of cargo pants as the Swiss army knife of clothing. After all, you may not *need* thirty-four pockets on your pants all the time, but wouldn't you rather have them and not need them than vice versa? And when we are outdoors, we can carry close to four days worth of supplies in those glorious pockets.

Pockets give us the perfect place to carry all of our man stuff. If we didn't have pockets, we'd probably all be wearing fanny packs. So thanks to the sewn-in pocket and the cargo pant for saving humanity from the horror of a world full of bag-wearing men.

BOXERS, BRIEFS, AND TIGHTY-WHITIES

In bedrooms around the world, a battle is being fought: the great boxers versus briefs debate. And today, a new entrant into the battle, boxer briefs, is also gaining a solid foothold in man world. Men want comfort, style, and functionality in the underwear department, and anything that delivers is a great manvention. But, unlike women, most men also refuse to spend much money on the underwear battle. It's just not necessary. We love our underwear and will wear them until someone (wife, girlfriend, mom) finally gets fed up with the holes and stains and tosses them out.

> **MAN-TASTIC FACT**
>
> **Long johns were named after legendary boxer John L. Sullivan who fought in them.**

The early days of male support ran from loincloths to codpieces to long johns. Long johns were favored by men in cold climates but not so practical in the heat, though the back flap was a welcome relief as you headed for the outhouse. Most men weren't happy about having to wear an entire set of undergarments under our clothes, but we had little choice until the twentieth century.

MAN-TASTIC FACT

Former Fed Chairman Alan Greenspan actually said that male underwear is an indicator of the economy. In good times, male undergarment sales spike. But in bad times, we men wear them until there is nothing left but an elastic band.

Tighty-whities were the hands-down winner of the battle after their introduction in the 1930s. The Y vent and support made them the choice for most men (and underwear-buying women). But then boxers entered the fray. Boxer shorts were designed after Everlast boxing shorts. In boxing, footwork is important, and boxer shorts give your legs a lot of freedom and they leave your boys hanging, which some guys love. In the 1990s, boxer briefs began to grab a solid foothold in men's departments. In a man's world, hanging free is good, but sometimes the boys need support. Boxer briefs add the look of a boxer, which surveys say women prefer, with the added bonus of the "pouch" to push big willie to the front. In fact, athletes often wear boxer briefs instead of a jock. After all, you don't want to be dangling, wangling, and wiggling on the basketball court. Boxer briefs

also eliminate that hated man issue of chafing. The battle rages on, but it is three-front war now, and for us men, it's a win-win situation.

BUILT-IN STADIUM CUP HOLDERS

If there's one thing that men enjoy it's sporting events. We love the sights and sounds of a live game—and with Jumbotrons we even get replays. Of course, food and drink is more expensive at the venue, but live games give us a chance to boo, cheer, and wear body paint. Going to a game in days of yore, say in the 1980s, had one major drawback: there wasn't anywhere to put our beer! Here necessity was the father of manvention, and the built-in cup holder was born.

Prior to the cup holder days, we had two choices: hold our beer or risk putting it on the ground. Neither choice was good. Holding our drink severely limited our chance to boo; it takes two hands to get the max sound we need when we are raining boos down on an opponent. And there are times in a man's life when you just have to boo a ref. Putting our drinks on the ground was also an iffy proposition, especially if you wanted to drink anymore. People on their way out of your aisle were invariably going to kick your beer over, and God only knows what could fly into your drink if it were on the ground. Luckily, the built-in cup holder showed up to save the day.

Cup holders are a great manvention. In fact, over 92 percent of all fans surveyed use the cup holders during games. At baseball games, we now have two hands to catch foul balls. At football games, we have two hands to do the wave. And at soccer games, we have one hand to flip off the opposing fans and one hand to hold a vuvuzela. But best of all, we are no longer going to spill our beer on other fans when a big play happens. Spilling a $12 beer is reason enough for a grown man to cry, and there's no crying in sports. So raise your beer in tribute to this wonderful manvention: the built-in cup holder.

VUVUZELAS

If you are going to cheer for your team, you want to get loud, and loud in the soccer world means vuvuzelas. Vuvuzelas leapt into the world's view at the 2010 World Cup, and men everywhere said, "Oh! Where can I get one of those?" Vuvuzelas are sure to be a staple of soccer crowd hooligans from now on, but they have been a staple of the South African soccer world for years.

MAN-TASTIC FACT

Hyundai built a vuvuzela over 100 feet long out of aluminum as a marketing ploy during the 2010 World Cup in Cape Town, South Africa. Town authorities forbade them from playing it out of health concerns.

Vuvuzelas look just like African horns that were used to call group meetings for centuries, and a similar-looking stadium horn was marketed in the United States in the 1960s. The 2010 World Cup games sounded like the stadiums were being infested with a plague of locusts due to their incessant, low-frequency buzzing sound. ESPN and the BBC even experimented with ways to filter out the sound for the home-viewing audience with mixed results. Soccer authorities even talked about banning them since soccer fans could use them as weapons. Seems a shame to me. Soccer is a man favorite because of the rowdy, obnoxious fans. You won't find a golf clap at a soccer match; you'll only hear in-your-face rooting for a favorite team. We men love cheering on our favorite teams, and vuvuzelas are just another weapon in our bag of annoying tricks. But be warned, many stadiums (like Yankee Stadium) are already moving to ban them.

But really, what's not to love? Heck, it only takes eleven cents of plastic to make one. And they can be made in all of your favorite team colors. And when you are done with the game, the vuvuzela makes a great beer funnel.

THUNDERSTICKS

The basketball equivalent to the vuvuzela is the thunderstick, a plastic, inflatable balloon that fans smack together to make a lot of noise. Thundersticks are also sold in team colors and help fans get loud. Clapping to make noise is hard work, so grab a set of this thunderous manvention and let the banging begin.

The people of Korea were the first to use thundersticks. Then their banging took the world by storm. After all, banging brings out the best in everybody. Thundersticks (sometimes called bambams, bangers, or thunderstix) were adopted in the United States by baseball and basketball teams. And in fact, basketball is the king of thunderstick sports. The closed arenas magnify the banging sound, and hundreds of thundersticks can also be waved behind the basket to distract the other players. Thundersticks are also popular on the political front; they make political rallies more fun. Loud, obnoxious, and fun, thundersticks are a great sports manvention.

MAN-DATE

Thor is the Norse god of thunder, lightning, strength, and fertility. The hammer-wielding dude is also one cool superhero created by Stan Lee in 1962.

MAN-TASTIC FACT

Thunder is created by the rapid expansion of air caused by the heat generated inside a lightning bolt.

Top Ten Best Manventions from the 1980s

1. Personal computers
2. Post-it Notes
3. Pac-Man
4. Spandex for women
5. Big hair
6. Cell phones
7. MTV
8. Members Only jackets
9. Game Boy
10. Leg warmers

CHAPTER 5

AUDIO AND VISUAL:

BECAUSE THE WORLD IS JUST BETTER WITH SURROUND SOUND

INSIDE THIS CHAPTER YOU WILL FIND:

- ☑ Yellow Lines in Football
- ☑ Jumbotrons
- ☑ Instant Replay and Slow Motion
- ☑ Surround Sound and Subwoofers
- ☑ 3-D TV
- ☑ HDTV
- ☑ ESPN
- ☑ The Sports Ticker
- ☑ DVRs
- ☑ Remote Controls, Three Channels, and Walking Across The Room

Men are visual people. And we have been blessed with many manventions that help us appreciate the visual world around us, including HDTV, yellow lines, instant replay, and *SportsCenter*. We also like to listen, so surround sound is another audiophile favorite. And no manvention is more cherished than the beloved remote control. So, tear yourself away from your 84-inch plasma TV for a few minutes as we explore the world of audio and visual stuff for men.

YELLOW LINES IN FOOTBALL

Men love watching sports, and in the past twenty years we have seen sports broadcasting evolve. But computers have been the biggest boon to our couch-watching sports pastime. And in no place have computers helped more than with the familiar yellow first-down line superimposed across the football field on our TV screens. The yellow line is one of the greatest sports manventions of the last twenty years.

The yellow line was first conceived in 1998, and now it would be almost impossible to live without it. We actually get a better view than the refs, and can clearly see that our favorite player made it because the football broke the yellow line. But the process that puts that yellow line there for our viewing pleasure is complicated. First, a three-dimensional virtual map of the field is created before the game (usually before the season). Football fields are not perfectly flat for drainage. An operator must input the exact yard line during the game, and the computer keeps it in the correct perspective on your home screen. But how do they get it yellow and not cut through the players? And how does it move as the camera moves?

The yellow line is created by a process called "chroma keying" (also called a green screen). The colors of the field are keyed into the computer, and only those colors are replaced with the yellow line. Your local weather bimbo uses the same process. She stands in front of a blank green screen and waves her arms. The computer replaces the green with the weather map. She must look to a monitor on the side to make sure she is pointing at the correct area. If she wore any green, the weather map would show up on

MAN-DATE

In 1996, Fox brought the idea of high tech to the world of hockey by introducing us to the "glow puck" (officially called the FoxTrax Puck). The puck contained electronic equipment that allowed it to show up on the TV screen surrounded by a glowing blue halo. On hard slap shots the puck would leave a long red comet's tail. To most hockey purists' delight, the glow puck was retired to the penalty box within two years.

the green clothing. But the football field is a little more complicated.

For one, the field is not just one shade of green, so several shades have to be keyed in. Second, as shadows move across the field (or it gets muddy), the colors have to be updated during the game. Also, a list of colors that are never replaced is keyed in. These include both teams' uniform colors, referees' uniform colors, and skin colors for the players.

The yellow line technology is now used in almost all sports for advertising and special graphics. For example, watch baseball and you might see an ad on the outfield grass. Auto racing adds in checkered strips at the finish line, and they can create graphics that move with the cars as they race. The process can also be used to embed a video right onto the screen within a picture. But the technology has been put to the best use in football. We now get a bonus as the running back struggles for a first down. Those men watching from home actually know if a player made it before the player does, at least right now. And if that's not a great manvention, I don't know what is.

JUMBOTRONS

Guys love going to see a live game, but for years going to a game meant giving up instant replays and slow motion. In the mid-eighties all that changed thanks to the Jumbotron. Now we can go to a game and still get almost all the comforts of home.

Jumbotrons were created by the Sony Corporation and premiered in 1985. Jumbotron is actually a registered trademark for Sony, even though they got out of the large-screen display business in 2001. The term is now universally applied by us common folk to all big-screen displays. Original Jumbotrons were essentially a series of picture tubes that were linked together to create a wall-sized picture, but today most jumbo display boards use LED (light-emitting diode) technology for long life and clarity.

MAN-DATE

In 2009, Cowboys Stadium opened in Dallas with the largest Jumbotron in the world. It is larger than eight full-size movie screens. The Cowboys Stadium Jumbotron is so big that it actually interferes with the field of play. Every punter in the NFL is capable of kicking a ball into it, if he wanted to.

We men now get the pleasure of seeing a game live and with replays. It is just like watching a game at home—on a TV the size of your house. Jumbotrons are also a hit with the players. They now get to check themselves out as the game goes on, and they get additional help when arguing with a referee. The whole crowd gets in on the action and gets to let their thoughts be known after a replay of a blown call.

Over the years, Jumbotrons have also shown up at concerts, which adds to the fun because we get to experience the joy of live music and we also get to see if our favorite star is hung over. With giant screens we can see all the detail of our favorite act. I saw the Rolling Stones years ago and was so far from the stage that Mick Jagger looked like a half-inch-tall mini rooster as he strutted around stage. Now with a Jumbotron, I could probably see his liver spots on the screen. And you could see that Keith Richards has actually pickled himself with all the drugs and liquor he has ingested over the years. The Jumbotron. Great for men. Not so great for rock stars.

INSTANT REPLAY AND SLOW MOTION

Now we have the Jumbotron, but it wouldn't do us any good without instant replay and the ability to see that instant replay in slow motion. We're always asking ourselves, *were the umpires right*? We also want the added benefit of seeing a play ten times in super-slow motion to debate the call. Whether we're at the game or at home, replays only add to our sports excitement—and they add to our TV viewing pleasure in other ways as well.

The Canadian Broadcasting Corporation premiered instant replay in 1955 for the insanely popular show "Hockey Night in Canada." George Retzlaff, the writer/producer of the show, used a "hot processor" to develop a film version of goals so they could be replayed within thirty seconds of the shot going in. Instant replay was born.

As magnetic videotaping became the norm (instead of film), instant replay exploded in the 1960s and 1970s for television sports. Referees and umpires hated instant replays (and most still do). They have about one-tenth of a second to make a call as the play happens, but we have the luxury of repeated slow-motion viewings to see how the umps blew the call. Many sports have incorporated video reviews into the game. We might as well use the technology if it exists. Basketball, baseball, tennis, hockey, and football all use video replay to some extent to help the umpires out.

Wouldn't it be great if we could extend instant replay into all facets of our lives? Most arguments could be ended with a slow-mo instant replay. Your wife argues with you and then sets the stage for a video challenge. If you're not sure what was said, you'd just go to the booth to find out. Now you can end any he said/she said argument with a red challenge flag. Of course, in order to do this, you'd need cameras rolling all the time, but with the popularity of reality TV, I'm sure there are a few ways to make that work.

SURROUND SOUND AND SUBWOOFERS

We love movies, and when we watch a movie, we want to be moved. I'm not talking emotionally moved here, I mean that we really want to be physically moved. We want to shake, rattle, and roll as the action is going on. And surround sound and subwoofers make that dream a reality. And we owe these wonderful manventions to fantasy, science fiction, and geeks.

MAN-DATE

Before *Close Encounters of the Third Kind* came out in 1977, Steve McQueen, Dustin Hoffman, Al Pacino, Gene Hackman, and Jack Nicholson all turned down the lead role.

We are naturally surrounded by noise and are able to hear and interpret sounds coming from all directions. But it's a little harder to duplicate this experience for TV, film, and music. Easy enough in concept, surround sound tries to recreate the way we naturally hear sound by sending different sounds to different speakers depending on what's going on in the movie, TV show, or song. That way, planes or cars traveling across the picture have accompanying sound that travels across the speakers, or sounds behind the character on the screen come out of the rear speakers so we hear it behind us as well. The first movie to use a form of surround sound was Walt Disney's (he's pretty famous) *Fantasia* in 1940. Disney used Fantasound to send four channels of music to different speakers, and the concept of surround sound was born.

But it was expensive, and since it only cost twenty-five cents to go to the movies, it didn't catch on. Quadraphonics (four speaker) systems showed up for music in the 1970s, but, frankly, they didn't work very well. It took a Dolby and a little sci-fi to make this manvention work.

The Dolby of surround sound fame is Ray, not Thomas Dolby and his nerd anthem "She Blinded Me with Science." The now legendary Dolby sound began in movie theaters, and it took two 1977 smash movies to take it to the masses. In the summer of 1977, *Star Wars,* where we first met Darth and his kids, Leia and Luke, was one of the first movies to use Dolby Stereo, the surround sound for movie theaters. Now, we men were sitting smack in the midst of a space battle with the sound of spaceships seemingly flying around and over us, and we loved it. In the fall of the same year, *Close Encounters of the Third Kind* also let us feel the music. Both were megahits, and soon men wanted nothing more than for Dolby sound to walk through the doors into our homes, which Dolby made possible with Dolby Pro Logic and Dolby Surround, the home versions of Dolby Stereo.

> **MAN-TASTIC FACT**
>
> **John Williams did the music for both *Star Wars* and *Close Encounters of the Third Kind*. Hell, Mr. Williams has done almost every blockbuster in the last forty years, including all the Harry Potter films, all the *Star Wars* films, and all the Indiana Jones movies just to name a few.**

The advent of home theater systems that began after these two movies made us men realize we needed to *feel* the movie, and nothing helps us do that more than a subwoofer, a giant speaker that pumps up the bass and is designed to play back a special audio channel (called the low-frequency effect channel) that has deep, low-pitched sounds. Now, when something explodes on the screen, you can actually feel the explosions because the subwoofer amplifies those extremely low notes and sound effects and rattles your furniture. Surround sound and subwoofers changed the way men watch movies, and home systems have grown bigger, more manly, and more expensive ever since.

3-D TV

As men know, size matters. And in the TV world, width and length have been the only two things we needed to concern ourselves with. But today, men now have to add depth to the discussion since the new generation of man-friendly TVs will almost all be 3-D. 3-D movies may have started as a gimmick (thanks *Avatar*), but now they are the hottest film technology, and if they can do something in the theaters it doesn't take long for men to want that same technology in their homes.

How does 3-D work? Well, our eyes allow us to see in 3-D all of the time. That is why a wet T-shirt contest during spring break is better than your *Playboy* collection. Each eye captures a separate image and your brain combines those two images into a well-rounded 3-D image. The trick with TVs is to send two images and let your brain put them back together. The easiest way is with the oh-so-funky 3-D glasses. By the way, GIs are issued those same glasses for computer simulation training and they have a great nickname for them: birth control glasses, or BCG. Men, you might want to stick to regular television when the ladies come over.

MAN-DATE

James Cameron wrote the original script for *Avatar* in the mid 1990s, but the technology to film it the way he envisioned it didn't yet exist. So he got to work on *Titanic*, the longest chick flick ever, in the meantime.

3-D glasses can use one of three technologies. Early style glasses (think 1950s and Disneyland) used a red filter and a blue filter to block out one image. Second-generation glasses used different polarized lenses for each eye (think *Avatar* and Disney World). The newest style uses a shutter that literally closes to block an image from getting to each eye. These glasses must be synchronized to the television set to work. But an even better method is coming.

In the world of better mousetraps, 3-D flat screens without glasses are on their way—and are actually already here if you have truckloads of cash. The future of non-butt-ugly-glass-wearing 3-D TV is lenticular displays. Lenticular displays use tiny lenses to direct one image to your left eye and one to your

right so that you see 3-D without glasses. The major drawback is you must be in the sweet spot (think front row center at that wet T-shirt contest). If you're even just a few degrees off the center line, the picture will just look fuzzy. But never fear, men will demand that the technology get better. After all, one advantage to home theater movie watching is that we can pause the movie if we get a better offer on the couch.

HDTV

Men are visual creatures. We like to watch anything and everything, from lingerie fashion shows to sporting events. And there is nothing out there that pays more homage to the chest-pounding-I-am-a-male viewer than high-definition television, or HDTV. HDTV is a manvention that will stand the test of time, primarily because it can just gain more high definition and still keep the acronym. And we owe it all to the Japanese and a grand alliance.

Standard television was developed in the 1920s and 1930s and made men happy. Of course, it was in black and white and the picture was very grainy, but at the time we didn't care. Then, in the 1960s, the Japanese began developing a system to put more definition in the picture. How did they do this? Well, all TV

> ***MAN-TASTIC FACT***
>
> Digital compression allows more information to be sent over the same bandwidth, and more information means more definition.

and computer screens are composed of individual dots (pixels) that make up the picture. HDTV just uses more dots, which leads to a clearer picture, and the clearer the better as far as men are concerned. Although the Japanese started the HDTV movement, it took TV-worshipping American men to take it to the next level. The grand alliance featured AT&T, General Instrument, MIT, Philips, Sarnoff, Thomson, and Zenith and put all of the U.S. HDTV research together and men started to rejoice; HDTV was soon available for the masses. Now, we had TV at home that rivaled movies in the theater and live sporting events.

It is almost painful to watch sports and movies on an old-fashioned set now. We worship our HDTV signal. We now can see every detail of a game, every blade of grass, every bleeding cut on the players, and every grimace of pain when our favorite player takes a shot to the nuts. Now we can create a home theater and reproduce a theater feel without $20 popcorn. And any time technology allows us to watch our favorite movies in our underwear, you know it's a great manvention.

ESPN

To many men, sports are meant to be revered. And nothing pays homage to sports like ESPN, the only place you can find sports of all kinds on twenty-four hours a day, seven days a week. And to think, we owe this unbelievable manvention to two guys getting fired. Bill Rasmussen and his son Scott both worked for the World Hockey Association's New England Whalers in the mid-1970s. Both were fired in 1977 and needed to find something else to do. Their loss was man's gain.

After being fired, the pair set out to broadcast local Connecticut sports over the satellite. They called the company Entertainment and Sports Programming network. According to company lore, the name was changed to ESPN when the letterhead came back from the printer with the N included in the logo. The Rasmussens found out it was cheaper to lease twenty-four blocks of time than the original five-hour time slots they sought. ESPN's twenty-four-hour signal was born and men rejoiced.

MAN-DATE

September 7, 1979, is a date that will be forever worshipped by men. This is the date the first *SportsCenter* was broadcast to launch ESPN on the air.

ESPN launched with an edition of *SportsCenter* followed by a pro softball game between the Milwaukee Schlitz and the Kentucky Bourbons. To add to the allure, the first large-scale advertiser was Budweiser. Beer, whiskey, and full-time sports programming was a match made in manvention heaven. The early days were filled with any sports that the company could get cheap. Aussie rules football, kick boxing, pro softball, and Irish hurling (a combination of lacrosse and field hockey) filled the airwaves in the early days of the network. ESPN even broadcast early games of March Madness in 1980 featuring the legendary finals showdown between Larry Bird and Magic Johnson.

ESPN also changed cable television forever when the company figured out a new way to make money. Prior to the early 1980s all of ESPN's income came from advertising revenue. The signal was provided to the cable companies for free. ESPN suggested charging cable companies a fee for each subscriber. The fee initially started at six cents per subscriber. Many cable companies balked, but men demanded full-time sports and ESPN took off. Premium cable networks now all charge a fee per subscriber.

ESPN deserves its rightful place in the pantheon of manventions, and virtually every man in the world would win *Name That Tune* if it started with the ubiquitous ESPN jingle. It sounds like the angels singing to most of us.

THE SPORTS TICKER

Men are impatient. We want instant knowledge (wireless internet anyone?). In the old days, scores would be updated every ten minutes, but today's men don't have an extra ten minutes, which makes the sports ticker (also called the sports crawl) a sports-loving couch potato's dream. We no longer have to channel flip (or log on) to keep up with everything else in the wide world of sports.

MAN-DATE

The stock ticker machine was used from 1870 until 1970. The ticker would transmit stock transactions over telegraph lines. With thousands of yards of used tape to get rid of, stock sellers started looking for any excuse to throw it out the window, and the ticker-tape parade was born. The first parade was thrown in 1886 to help celebrate the dedication of the Statue of Liberty.

ESPN was one of the first television networks to run a continual crawl across the bottom of the screen. Tickers are common on almost all news stations now, giving us info on everything from sports, weather, and news, but ESPN was first. Of course, they take up a few precious inches of screen, but men don't care. It helps that we all have 84-inch plasma screens nowadays, so losing a few inches still gives us plenty. Just imagine the sports crawl on a dinosaurish 13-inch screen; you'd need binoculars to read it from the easy chair. Honestly, though, we want instant news so much—especially when it has to do with sports—that we'd probably love it anyway.

DVRS

Digital video recorders (DVRs) make us glad to be men. Miss a play? Rewind and watch it again. Need a trip to the throne? Pause and pick up where you left off later. The best part is we can get back to live TV by skipping commercials (can I get an amen from the men in the room?).

As most men already know, the DVR is a giant hard drive designed to record whatever you want. No tapes or discs to buy ever. Size matters, so you have a maximum amount of man stuff you can record, but most DVRs allow you to capture at least 300 hours of TV. But one of the best features is that the DVR will record even things you didn't know you'd want. The DVR always records all the signal in a buffer usually one hour in length, so if you missed the last goal of the Stanley Cup Finals because you were making a beer run, it's not a problem. Rewind and you can see the goal and jump back to where you were. Need to pause live TV? Go right ahead. The DVR captures a freeze frame of where you stopped the show, just as if you paused an old VCR tape, but the machine keeps recording the live action. Since it is a digital recording, you can pick up right where you left off when you return.

MAN-DATE

TiVo (the first DVR on the planet) was set to be shipped on March 31, 1999. Since that date was a blue moon (second full moon in a month), the TiVo engineers code-named the project Blue Moon.

Most DVRs also give you the option of recording anything starring a certain actor or a genre of film. Want all of the sci-fi films ever made, just DVR sci-fi films and your hard drive will fill up within a week. A sneakier use for a DVR is to set your friend's DVR to record stuff he won't like. You can record musicals for that sports-loving über-jock. Or you can record sports for your musical-loving best friend. DVRs makes all of your favorite things possible: pausing live TV, skipping commercials, and screwing with your friends.

REMOTE CONTROLS, THREE CHANNELS, AND WALKING ACROSS THE ROOM

The beloved remote control, the little invention that keeps us glued to the couch. We love the pleasure of scanning through three hundred channels. We cry in agony when the remote slips into the depths of the couch. We are spoiled and we love it. And just think, we owe one of the greatest manventions of all time to a toy sailboat.

Remote controls were actually the brainchild of famed inventor Nikola Tesla. In about 1900, he used his remote control to power a toy boat that he could sail on lakes around his house. Little did he know that his invention had the power to turn us into couch potatoes.

MAN-TASTIC FACT

Commercials have gotten shorter and faster paced since the advent of the remote control. In the 1950s, commercials were leisurely paced and would often last a minute or more. Men didn't have much choice without a remote. Now commercials run between fifteen to thirty seconds and are faster paced in a vain attempt to keep our interest.

The first long-distance remote controls weren't actually that remote. The Lazy Bones was introduced by Zenith (then called the Zenith Radio Company) in 1950. It was attached to the set by a cord. It soon disappeared off the market for safety reasons. Then, in walked Zenith engineers Robert Adler and Eugene Polley. Polley developed the Flashmatic remote control, a true remote since it didn't have a cord. This remote actually used a flashlight aimed at a photocell on the front of the set. Unfortunately, the photocell couldn't distinguish the remote light from other lights in the room. Open a curtain, you would change your channel. Turn on a lamp and the volume would go up. These remotes soon went the way of the dodo as well. It would take a mini xylophone to create the modern day remote control.

In 1956, Robert Adler developed the Space Commander 600 remote control. This clever remote actually worked without batteries. The remote had a mini xylophone inside, and hitting a button caused a tiny hammer to strike an aluminum rod. The vibrations were different for every button since the rods were different lengths. The ultrasonic sounds were picked up by the set and the channel or the volume would change depending on what button you hit. These ultrasonic signals were the basis of remote controls for the next twenty years. You still had to step through the channels to change them, but let's be honest, there were only three channels at the time.

MAN-DATE

In 1997, Adler and Polley garnered an Emmy Award for making us men into couch potatoes.

Today's remote controls use either infrared (IR) light or radio signals. The IR remote has a light-emitting diode on the front of the remote that blinks very fast, sending a particular signal (depending on which button you push on the remote) to the sensor on the set. Each signal has a different meaning: channel up, volume down, turn to channel 156, and so on. The IR remotes still have one drawback: they need line-of-sight access to function properly. If your kid stands in front of the sensor, the remote won't work.

Radio frequency (RF) remotes eliminate the need for line-of-sight access since the radio waves travel through and around most things like children. Funny thing, Zenith actually wanted to use radio signals in the 1950s but scrapped the idea since you could change your neighbor's TV channel through the walls. Today, the signals are coded so that your remote only controls one set.

Remote controls are one of the definitive manventions of the last one hundred years. The co-inventors definitely deserve a sitting ovation.

Top Ten Best Manventions from the 1990s

1. The Internet
2. PlayStation
3. The Wonderbra
4. Extreme sports
5. DVDs
6. Viagra
7. Energy drinks
8. *Beavis and Butthead*
9. Wi-Fi
10. The Spice Girls

CHAPTER 6

COMPUTERS AND TECHNOLOGY:

MEN LOVE TO LOG ON

INSIDE THIS CHAPTER YOU WILL FIND:

- ☑ The Snooze Button
- ☑ Ctrl-Alt-Delete
- ☑ YouTube
- ☑ iPods, iPhones, and iPads
- ☑ Google
- ☑ Social Networking
- ☑ Mafia Wars

There's something about new technology that men just love. If it's a cutting-edge gadget, we want it and we want it now. We're all about instant gratification, and now, thanks to technology, everything we want is at the tip of our fingers. So, take a load off and enjoy yourself as we explore the marvelous manventions that have come to us via computers and technology.

THE SNOOZE BUTTON

There's nothing like a good night's sleep. You're warm. You're cozy. You're in the middle of a dirty dream. And then you're startled awake by that hated alarm buzz. Fortunately, one of man's favorite manventions is here to give you those much-needed additional ten minutes that will make your life that much easier. The snooze button is an early morning godsend, but it took its sweet time getting to its favorite spot at your bedside.

Alarm clocks are old. The Greeks had a crude alarm clock in 250 B.C. that used rising water to cause an alarm to go off at a prescribed time. Levi Hutchins built the first mechanical alarm clock in 1787. The drawback to his invention was that it only went off at 4 A.M. Levi was an early riser, so he built a clock to wake him up at that ungodly hour. But he never patented his invention. The first fully adjustable alarm clock to get a patent was in 1876, by the Seth Thomas company, which was one of the best-known clock companies at the time.

> **MAN-TASTIC FACT**
>
> Roosters crow at any time of the day or night, not just in the morning. They crow when startled. They crow when looking for love. They crow in response to other crowing. Perhaps we are only annoyed in the early morning because they wake us up.

In the good old days (like the 1950s), hitting the snooze button would give you an extra nine minutes of sleep. These clocks used gears to keep time, and clockmakers slid in a gear that would change after nine minutes had elapsed. Fortunately, today's digital clocks can be set with any snooze length, which is perfect for those who want to gradually face the day—or finish that dream where we're rubbing suntan oil on that Hawaiian Tropic swimsuit model. What a way to face the day!

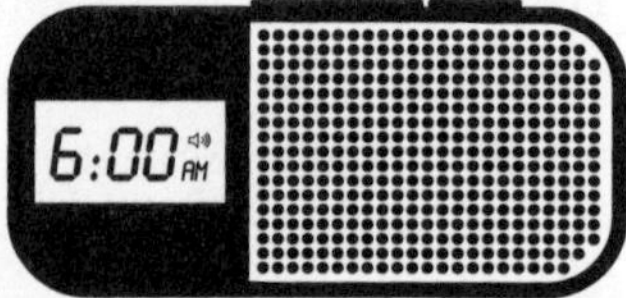

CTRL-ALT-DELETE

The computer is an amazing manvention that makes it easy for men to do the things we need, like pay bills, communicate with our buds, and surf the Net for useless information. Heck, some of us have even found love on a computer. But occasionally our computers let us down, and that's when Ctrl-Alt-Delete comes into play.

You may have noticed that computers only crash at the most inopportune times. Like when you are just about to bid in an online auction or when you are IMing a possible new lady friend. What do men do when our computers freeze? We first try to close the program, only to be greeted with the "program is not responding" message. Don't you just love that message? It kind of states the obvious. We wouldn't be closing the program if it were working. So then what do we do? If we are using a PC, we give the machine a salute. First, a one-fingered salute accompanied by your favorite cuss words in triplicate. Then, we give the computer the three-finger salute.

The three-finger salute is done by pressing the Ctrl-Alt-Delete keys at the same time. In older Windows versions this forces the machine to do a soft reboot. In newer versions it brings up the task manager, which allows you to close the nonresponding program.

David Bradley, one of the original designers of the IBM PC, first implemented Ctrl-Alt-Delete. The choice of keys was designed for it to be impossible to do accidentally. Two Shift keys are on one end of the keyboard, and the Delete key is at the opposite end. The three-fingered salute has been a staple for anyone who has spent any time using a PC, but the keystroke wasn't originally intended for us web surfers. It was designed for programmers. When writing new code, you have to continually reboot whenever you get stuck. But soon the salute was released to the general public, and we have used it ever since.

MAN-TASTIC FACT

The Boy Scouts also have a three-fingered salute using the middle three fingers of their right hand. The three fingers represent honoring God, helping others, and obeying the Scout Law. Most older men in the U.S. also have a one-finger salute for use while driving, playing sports, and just hanging out with our buds.

YOUTUBE

Men like to watch, and the perfect place to watch anything is YouTube. Want to see someone light something on fire? Want to see a girl snort a piece of spaghetti and then regurgitate it out her mouth? Want to see how to change a water pump on a 1978

Pacer? It's all up there on YouTube, which is one of the three most-visited websites on the planet—and we owe it all to a trio of very rich twentysomethings.

The publicly floated story is that the idea for YouTube came after a dinner party with Steve Chen, Chad Hurley, and Jawed Karim. They had trouble sharing videos of the evening over the computer, and the idea for YouTube was born. That story is simple and popular but also probably wrong. One of the cofounders says the party never happened. Maybe he just had *too* much of a good time. But the trio did find a way to allow anybody to upload videos of anything, at any time. Of course, this seems normal to us now, but it was a breath of fresh air back in the stone age of 2005.

The boys cashed out (less than two years later) and sold the company to Google for more than $1.5 billion. And we know where we can find videos of absolutely everything. It just doesn't get any better than that.

MAN-DATE

The first video ever loaded onto YouTube is an eighteen-second clip of YouTube creator Jawed Karim at the San Diego Zoo. He explains that elephants have very long trunks.

IPODS, IPHONES, AND IPADS

Show me a man who doesn't love gadgets and . . . well, I just don't think that man exists. Men love gadgets. And ever since 2001, Apple has been the company we go to for state-of-the-art gadgetry. Just slap a little *i* in front of anything and you can guarantee that soon it will be flying off the shelves, and, for that we can thank everyone's favorite nerd: Steve Jobs.

Jobs is the epitome of techno-cool. And when he talks, men listen (and open their wallets). In the fall of 2001, he walked up on stage and set the world on its ear with his introduction of the first iPod. Now it was possible for you to have a thousand tunes right at your fingertip in a cool (and tiny), magical musical box. MP3 players were already on the market, but the iPod was backed by the mega-company Apple, and those things sold. Over the next few years, Apple shrunk them and made them more user friendly. But nerd boy wasn't done.

After all, if a mini music player would sell, why not add a phone to the mix? They did, and the iPhone was born. Jobs made this announcement in 2007, and our wallets opened again. Now we had an ultra-cool touch-screen phone that could browse the web and play music, too. But all of the apps that were created for it really caused the iPhone to explode. You can get apps for everything from making your

MAN-TASTIC FACT

Vinnie Chieco, a freelance copywriter, was hired by Apple to work with a team to introduce the unnamed musical device. When he first saw the white prototype, he thought of the movie *2001: A Space Odyssey* and the line "Open the pod bay doors, HAL." In the movie, the pod was free to dock and undock from the ship, just as an iPod docks and undocks from a computer. The team just added an *i* to the front and a legend was born.

own sushi to playing name that tune with music you hear on the radio. But the best was yet to come.

In 2010, Jobs opened his mouth about the iPad and more than 3 million sold in the first two months. The iPad is essentially just an iPhone on steroids or a notebook computer on crack cocaine. Many experts think the iPad will revolutionalize the way we read magazines, newspapers, books, and so on. And honestly, they're just really fun to play with. Apple and nerd boy have done us men proud.

GOOGLE

Back in the day, if you wanted to know something, you had to actually go to the library and look it up in a book, and, damn, is that hard work. Need the latest sports scores? Interested in a new woman? Want to see hot models in string bikinis? Now, all you have to do is go to Google and anything you want to know is there at your fingertips. This manvention has taken over the search engine world—and now they are after the e-mail world, too.

Google was started by two Stanford grad students, Larry Page and Sergey Brin, who were doing a project that they nicknamed BackRub. The goal of the project was to rank websites by the

MAN-DATE

Google, Inc. was incorporated in 1998. The first headquarters was in a garage.

MAN-TASTIC FACT

The word *google* was added to the Webster's dictionary in 2006.

number of other websites they were linked to. The more linked you were, the higher your page would rank. The pair was only trying to help academics at first, then they brought Google to the masses and never looked back. Today, Google has destroyed the other search engines (anybody remember Dogpile?) and has become a household name.

SOCIAL NETWORKING

Ever wondered what happened to that girl you dated in high school or that guy you hung out with in college? Forget Christmas cards or even e-mails. Today, we have the amazing manvention that is social networking. Facebook, MySpace, and Twitter keep us connected to people ranging from those we see on a daily basis to those we barely know and hardly care about. It's kind of voyeuristic, but we love it anyway.

The king of the social networking sites right now is Facebook, which is not bad for a website that didn't even exist until 2004. Mark Zuckerberg was a sophomore at Harvard when he started "Thefacebook," later shortened to just "Facebook." He had already developed a few social sites at Harvard, such as Coursematch (which did what you think) and Facemash (which got him in trouble). Facemash let students rank the attractiveness of other Harvard students, but Zuckerberg never asked to use the pictures, which was a big no-no in Beantown. Harvard didn't throw him out over the incident, but he eventually left to further develop Facebook.

MySpace predated Facebook by over a year and was actually initially more popular because it had better backing up front. Today, MySpace is popular amongst kids, but Facebook—which appeals to older users—is the world's top social networking site.

But as much as men love Facebook, we love Twitter even more. Twitter is even newer and faster and it gives men a great way to get instant info from our friends. A deck of cards and money to lose? Tweet. Hot girls at the pub? Tweet. Constant updates of bowel movements and random stuff can get annoying, but it keeps us in constant contact with our friends. CNN, ESPN, and Fox News love Twitter because overrated celebs, showboating athletes, and aspiring politicos tweet all the time. If you have twenty-four hours to fill with news or sports, you need something to talk about. Twitter keeps us instantly locked in to our friends and gives us stuff to laugh about on the news/sports channels. Men like to be locked into the latest info.

MAN-DATE

How do you get a college named after you? For John Harvard, it took the pricey sum of $1,000 and 400 books. Hey, it was 1638 and a thousand bones was a lot of money. Of course, they named it in his honor after he was dead.

Do you know what the next big website is? I don't either, but I bet some college student is already working on it.

MAFIA WARS

Men love gangsters. Who hasn't at least dreamed of building a criminal empire? You can't do it in real life because you will eventually get caught, but now we can pretend to be hard-core criminals without having to worry about dropping the soap. Just play Mafia Wars.

With a little help from your friends on Facebook and MySpace you can now earn your way up the Mafia ladder. You start out as a lowly street thug and work your way up to be a criminal mastermind by whacking your enemies and stealing whatever you can get your hands on. If you invest the time, you'll be constantly leveling up and gaining power. Mafia Wars even has several different versions of the game; if you want to rule the roost in Dublin, Bangkok, New York, or Cuba, you're good to go. So enjoy this kick-ass manvention . . . just don't get caught playing at work.

MAN-DATE

Although Al Capone and John Dillinger were both called Public Enemy Number One, neither was ever on the FBI's Top Ten Most Wanted List. The FBI's top ten list didn't start until 1950.

Top Ten Manventions You Must Google

1. Merkins
2. Radioactive jock strap
3. Prostate warmer
4. Lawson's Vaginal Washer
5. Comfort Wipe
6. Heidelberg electric belt
7. Gas mask bra
8. Smell-O-Vision
9. Spermatic Truss
10. Radium Ore Revigator

CHAPTER 7

FUN AND GAMES:

"YES, FANTASY FOOTBALL ISN'T REAL, BUT THAT DOESN'T MEAN WE DON'T WANT TO WIN"

INSIDE THIS CHAPTER YOU WILL FIND:

- ☑ The Super Soaker
- ☑ Fantasy Football
- ☑ Wii
- ☑ XBox 360
- ☑ Guitar Hero
- ☑ Pong and the Atari 2600
- ☑ Rock-Paper-Scissors
- ☑ No-Limit Hold'em
- ☑ Nude Playing Cards
- ☑ Firecrackers

Men live for the thrill of crushing an opponent, which is why we love sports so much. But we don't just want our sports teams to win; we want to win on our own, too. From backyard water battles to poker to video games, we live in a competitive world, and we'll compete for anything that we can possibly compete for: women, jobs, you name it; virtually everything in our lives is hard won. So put down the controller as we delve into the world of fun and games.

THE SUPER SOAKER

If you know anything about men, you know that we like extremes. Yes, a single-burner gas grill will cook a steak just fine, but a seven-foot-long, twelve-burner stainless steel grill is much cooler to stand in front of. An old Honda Civic will get you around town, but a Lamborghini can get you there much quicker (215 mph, anyone?).

> **MAN-TASTIC FACT**
>
> The original name of the Super Soaker was the Power Drencher. I guess it's a personal preference. Would you rather be soaked or drenched?

Nowhere in the world of backyard entertainment is this love of extremes more evident than during a water fight. Yes, men love things that are over the top, but we also like to win, and no one is going to win a water fight with a run-of-the-mill squirt gun. Enter the Super Soaker—an engineer's gift to backyard warriors.

The idea for the Super Soaker was developed in 1982 by engineer Lonnie Johnson. Johnson was doing some hydraulic design work and realized that he was close to inventing a water pistol to put all squirt guns to shame. All he needed to do was find a way to move more water. He experimented until he got just the right combination of air pressure and force. The result? A squirt gun powered by the entire arm, not just one little finger. Sounds extreme, right?

When you use a normal, plain Jane, run-of-the-mill squirt gun, you use your finger to create pressure and propel the water, but fingers have limited strength. Super Soakers have a handgrip and are powered by your entire arm, which generates more force and moves more water . . . a lot more water. Just think of a Super Soaker as a water rifle, not a water pistol.

In the world of building a better mousetrap, variations of the Super Soaker have added battery power to increase the power and even backpacks to increase the water supply. Awesome, right? All these variations and the total kick-assedness of the Super Soaker help it earn a place of honor as one of the top manventions of all time, and millions of wet, sunburnt, overstimulated men agree.

FANTASY FOOTBALL

Men find ways to compete even when other people are actually doing the sweating, and fantasy football is a way for a regular Joe to compete in the pro football world. And we get to do it without the chance of being chased by a three-hundred-pound freak of nature intent on separating our head from our body. And the best part about fantasy football is talking trash to our friends—and hoping our players back us up.

> ***Man-tastic Fact***
>
> **Over 30 million men play fantasy football online, and countless more play it in their offices.**

MAN-DATE

On October 29, 2009, the FX channel debuted a new series called *The League*, a comedy series about a fantasy football league. The stars of the show, along with the creators, play in a fantasy league that you can follow online. Google it and take a look.

We owe the invention of fantasy football to Oakland businessman and part owner of the Oakland raiders, Bill Winkenbach. On a road trip with the team in 1962, Bill decided that he and his buddies would pick pro football players and let their stats compete, and fantasy football was born. Fantasy football had a nice quiet run for about thirty years, and then the growth of the Internet caused the sport to explode. Now, it is easy to change lineups and get the latest rumors on players. Large TVs and computer graphics also helped because you can now be continually updated on stats via the sports crawl across the bottom.

Fantasy football is also really easy, which appeals to the casual fan. You can play fantasy anything, but football requires the least amount of time and dedication. After draft day, which is a great excuse to hang out with your buds and talk trash, all you need is a few minutes to set your lineup. Then sit back and watch your fantasy come to life.

WII

It is no secret that men love video games; any man under the age of fifty grew up gaming. But it took Nintendo and the Wii, our next great manvention, to get us gamers off the couch. Wii also made gaming more of a social activity and got many of us playing with our kids. Family reunion getting stale? Just bowl a few games with Grandma. Nephew bored? Just strike him out in baseball.

What makes the Wii so different from its competitors? Well, the Wii controller uses accelerometers and infrared tracking to supplement the traditional button-pushing of most controllers. The controller speaks to the Wii system and lets it know where you are and what you're doing. Those actions are then relayed into the game where you can watch yourself as a Mii (a Wii avatar) doing the same actions.

Wii has also created a whole market for exergaming. It started with boxing and has grown to include Wii Fit and Wii Sport. For both of these games, you use the Wii Balance Board—Wii's little way of making sure you're not playing from the couch. Now, we can tone up while never leaving the house, and anything that lets me do that is okay in my book.

MAN-DATE

Prior to 2006, the Wii was actually called the Revolution by Nintendo. The name was changed to make it universal throughout the world and promote the idea that two people would stand together to play many of the games.

XBOX 360

Playing against a computer is fun, but playing against another brain is better for most men. Most of the time it's actually easier to play against actual people anyway. To fulfill this desire, Xbox 360 and Xbox LIVE combined to give men an adrenalin rush and become a giant, fun, time suck. Now, we could fire up the game against real competition twenty-four hours a day.

Xbox 360 was released in 2005 from the megacompany Microsoft and is the oldest game system in the current market (PlayStation 3 and the Wii came out a year later). But older is better and wiser in some cases (just look at Demi Moore). Xbox 360 gives you over 1,000 games to choose from, which is more than its competitors offer. Xbox 360 was also the first to bring high definition video into the gaming world. But the 360 really amps up men because of the way it connects you to other players worldwide through its online connection, Xbox LIVE. Want to play Halo at 3 A.M.? You're in luck; a bevy of willing competitors exist. Want to crush a ten-year-old's ego at Madden? Just log on.

MAN-TASTIC FACT

Grand Theft Auto IV is thought to have cost more than $100 million to develop and market.

Xbox 360 has garnered a firm foothold in most men's worlds. And now with the Xbox 360's controllerless, full-body sensor (called Kinect) that totally immerses you in a game, be prepared to play twenty-four hours a day. Yeah, maybe you should be sleeping, but isn't the thrill of victory more fun?

GUITAR HERO

There's something about rock music that makes men want to let their hair down and let loose. Earlier on we discussed how much men love to play the air guitar. We hear a favorite guitar riff, and we toss our head around like Angus Young of AC/DC and strum away. It's pretty awesome. But, in 2005, we were finally given a way to put our highly developed air guitar skills to use via a little game called Guitar Hero.

MAN-TASTIC FACT

Did you know real-life rockers helped usher in Guitar Hero? Greg LoPiccolo and Eric Brosius, both of the nineties Boston band Tribe, were on the team responsible for Guitar Hero.

RedOctane was primarily developing controllers for full-size arcade games. After working on a full-size video game with a guitar, the company started building a smaller version for the home game market. They budgeted a paltry $1 million to develop the first game. A very wise use of money, don't you think? Now, any guy could attain guitar god status. Even fat-fingered men could play the guitar like the best of them. And the best part? We got to destroy our friends while doing it. We could even don a bandana and leather pants and look the part while we played. Guitar Hero allows us to be rock demons, and for that the game is considered one bad-ass manvention.

PONG AND THE ATARI 2600

Video games serve several functions. We use games to compete and trash talk. Sometimes we use them to unwind with a little mindless fun. I secretly use video games to procrastinate. If I am staring at a task I don't want to do, I grab a controller and lose myself for a little while. We just love to play. The feel of a controller in our hands gives us joy. But the game that started it all was a table-tennis video game named Pong.

Ralph Baer developed a table-tennis game for Magnavox. Upon playing the Magnavox game, Nolan Bushnell was inspired to create an arcade version of the game that he called Pong. He founded the company Atari to build the first one. A prototype of Pong was placed in a Stanford area bar and was an instant hit. Just drop in a quarter and you could be an electronic table-tennis god. After a few days though, it stopped working. Atari workers soon realized why it stopped: it was jammed full of quarters from overuse. The stand-up video game industry was born. But, in the mid-1970s, the game came home.

> ***MAN-TASTIC FACT***
>
> **The all-time best-selling game for the Atari 2600 was Pac-Man.**

The year was 1975. The president of the United States had just resigned, disco was just starting to rule the music scene, and bell bottom pants were the latest clothing craze. But the best part of 1975 was the release of a game called Home Pong. For those of you who have never seen one, Home Pong had dial knobs. The knobs were the first video game controllers, and, unlike today's controllers, they weren't wireless or on long cables. Instead, they were permanently attached to a box about the size of a New York City phone book. Home Pong plugged directly into the TV, and so did a variety of subsequent games. The market was crying out for a system that would work with more than one game. Enter the Atari 2600.

The Atari 2600 is like the father to all of our current video game systems. It was the first mass-marketed game to include game cartridges, which allowed us to just plug in another game when we got tired of what we were playing. The cartridges looked like mini clips for an assault rifle and plugged into the console. They had one thousandth of the memory of your average cell phone, but they gave us the freedom to change our minds on what game to play, and many of the Atari 2600 games, such as Asteroids, Defender, Space Invaders, and Frogger, are legendary. Atari 2600 also gave us our first look at sports games.

MAN-DATE

Credited by most as the father of video games, Nolan Bushnell was the founder of the Atari game company. He sold Atari in 1982 and founded another company that kids love and parents hate: Chuck E. Cheese.

Atari Football was a riot with its square football. And the football just stuck to the side of the square player's body. The playbook was limited, too. You had about ten plays to choose from, which was fine because you only had four players anyway. Baseball was also a blast. Learning how to hit a square ball was a challenge my Little League coach never taught me.

From 1975 up to now, home video games have been a kid's—and a man's—best friend. Pong started a revolution, and the Atari 2600 continued the party. This game and gaming system deserve a space of honor in the manvention top ten list even if you never played with either. After all, without Pong, there would be no Madden, Call of Duty, or Super Mario. And we can thank the Atari 2600 for the development of the Xbox, PlayStation, Sega, and Wii.

ROCK-PAPER-SCISSORS

Want to go first in a game? Rock-Paper-Scissors (RPS). Want to settle a bet? RPS. Want to decide a line call in a close game of tennis? RPS. Want to sell your multimillion-dollar art collection? RPS. Hard to believe, but it's true. In 2005, Takashi Hashiyama, president of Maspro Denkoh Corporation, called upon the ancient art of RPS to decide whether Sotheby's or Christie's would sell his company's $20 million art collection. The auction went to Christie's when they threw scissors to win the game. Millions of people throughout the world have been making decisions with this simple manvention for years.

Rock-Paper-Scissors is the ultimate way to settle any and all arguments. There's no equipment needed, just two hands and a little strategy. The game has been tested on playgrounds for years: rock breaks scissors, scissors cuts paper, paper smothers rock. Many people play best two out of three. Various cultures lay claim to the game. The Japanese have been playing a version called *jan-ken-pon* for centuries, and *rochambeau* and Paper-Scissors-Stone are other names that have been bandied about over the years. Perhaps we should have an RPS contest and once and for all decide the actual official name.

MAN-DATE

Modern cross-bladed scissors were invented in Italy sometime around 100 A.D.

Various RPS championships are played throughout the world every year, and, in fact, our favorite playground decider has become its own game with world champions. A word of advice: Never challenge a world champion for the next round of beers at your local pub. You'll lose every time. Books on strategy are available for the novice, but the best way to learn is just play until you get a feel for it. Practice makes perfect.

NO-LIMIT HOLD'EM

Hear the word *poker* and immediately think of guys sitting around the table drinking beer and moving money. And that's exactly why men love it. But today's poker game has come a long way from the dining-room table. Today, poker has exploded. It's everywhere—even on TV—and we owe it all to a tiny camera.

MAN-TASTIC FACT

It is impossible to make a straight in poker without having a five or a ten in your hand.

Poker has gained a following on television because of the pocket cameras that allow you, the viewer, to see all of the players' cards. A pocket cam is just a lipstick-sized camera mounted under the table to allow the home viewer to see the cards. We can also see the odds for each hand winning right there on the little screen, which makes the game much more fun. We stare in amazement as an idiot with pocket twos raises against a full house. (Really? What kind of idiot raises on pocket twos?) We watch a player go all-in and then walk away from the table with his head down when he loses, and then we revel in the fact that we would never do that. Many of us have even played Texas Hold'em just to emulate the pros. Usually, a few hands in, we wish we had pocket cams on our table for us to view. It would be cheating, but at least we wouldn't lose.

MAN-DATE

In 1970, seven players participated in the inaugural World Series of Poker Tournament at Binion's Horseshoe Casino. They played five different poker games, and in a secret vote by the players, Johnny Moss was named World Champion Poker Player. The next year the tournament was changed to No-Limit Texas Hold'em to determine the champ. Moss won again.

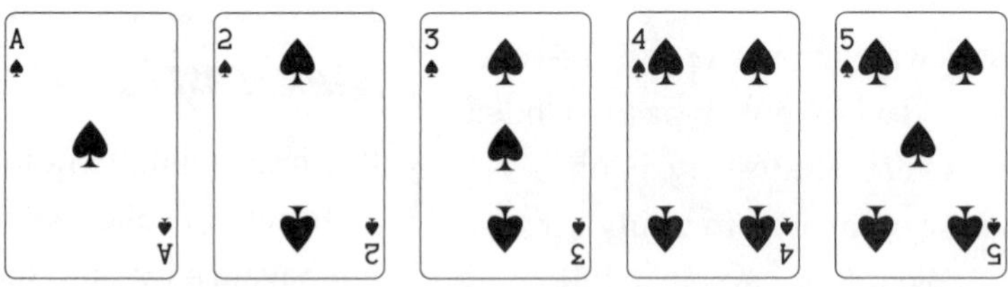

No-Limit Texas Hold'em tournaments dot the landscape now. Every casino has them, and you can't surf your TV channels without finding one. But why has No-Limit taken over the poker world? Two words: all in. No-Limit is the perfect game for liars, con men, psychologists, and anybody who is real good at reading people. The game is for bluffers. It's like playing the lottery; most people lose, but someone is going home rich, and men love the thought of going home rich, which is why we play in the first place. And, after all, we also know that we would never raise pocket twos against a full house.

NUDE PLAYING CARDS

Playing cards have been around for centuries and have provided men with hours of entertainment. From the early days of family games all the way to today's multimillion-dollar poker tournaments, playing cards are a welcome manvention—and they're even more welcome when you throw a little nudity into the mix.

Playing cards were most likely invented in China since paper was invented there, but several cultures lay claim to those beloved cards. But no matter where they were invented, the original cards were made by hand and were very expensive. The only people who could afford them were royalty (all of us "I'm going to lose all my money to my friends" guys were out of luck). Modern playing cards owe their ancestry to Europe, and it was the Europeans who based their cards on noble people: kings, queens, and knaves represented the face cards. Knave was too close to king and was eventually replaced by the jack. Until the 1800s, kings were always the high card. In the 1800s, some card games were played "ace high" and the ace became the boss card. Many people speculate "ace high" came from the French Revolution and symbolized the lower class being in power, but these claims are sketchy.

The four suits featured today on most cards in the Western world are also a European invention, but it's likely that they were at least inspired by Egyptian cards. The Egyptian cards (similar to tarot cards) contained polo sticks, coins, swords, and cups. In England this evolved into hearts, spades, diamonds, and clubs. The joker was a purely American invention to play the game Euchre in the 1800s.

One type of playing card makes poker night with the guys—or even a game of solitaire—a lot more appealing: the nude woman playing card. Everything's a lot more fun when you add in naked women. When you're looking at a picture of a woman with a stacked deck, you don't care so much that you just lost $100 to your best friend's obnoxious brother-in-law. Another good thing is that the women on the face cards are usually the best looking of the bunch. Kind of makes having a royal flush even better. Ah, the male mind at work.

FIRECRACKERS

Very little brings men more joy than the pyrotechnic spectacle that lighting a pack of firecrackers brings. Yes, firecrackers can be dangerous, but that—along with the flames and the ear-splitting noise—is just one of the reasons that they're such a great manvention. The sparking fuse is just a hint at the bit of backyard mayhem that we use to celebrate the Fourth of July, New Year's Day, Halloween, weddings . . . hell, we'll use firecrackers to celebrate any day that ends in Y. I even used to use firecrackers as an alarm clock for my college roommate. So I see nothing wrong with lighting a few to celebrate the invention of this great manvention.

The Chinese were the gunpowder kings long before most other civilizations. The weird thing is the first Chinese firecrackers didn't even contain gunpowder. Early firecrackers were created by tossing green bamboo into fires (and the Chinese have tons of bamboo).

MAN-TASTIC FACT

A squib is a small firecracker-like device used in movie special effects to simulate gunfire hitting walls, cars, and the ground. Just like modern dynamite, most are electrically detonated.

The segments of bamboo would heat up until they exploded open. These firecrackers were fun, but gunpowder gave them more bang and took them to a whole other level.

The Chinese were daring enough to pack gunpowder inside green bamboo segments, just to see what would happen. The result? The true firecracker was born. Over the years, firecrackers have morphed from powder-laden sticks of bamboo into tiny encased cardboard bombs that are safer and easier to control, which, for an exploding manvention, is a very good thing.

THE TOP TEN MANVENTIONS FROM THE 2000S

1. Low-rise jeans
2. Smartphones
3. Chuck Norris jokes
4. Flat-screen TVs
5. Bleached hair for dudes
6. Text messaging
7. DVD screens in cars
8. Mentos and Diet Coke
9. Bluetooth
10. Livestrong bracelets

CHAPTER 8

TOOLS AND HOUSEHOLD GADGETS:

MORE POWER + MORE TESTOSTERONE = MORE MAN TIME IN THE GARAGE

INSIDE THIS CHAPTER YOU WILL FIND:

- ☑ THE SWISS ARMY KNIFE
- ☑ TWO-IN-ONE SHAMPOO AND CONDITIONER
- ☑ GAS-POWERED LEAF BLOWERS, SNOW BLOWERS, AND WEED WHACKERS
- ☑ AIR CONDITIONING
- ☑ LA-Z-BOYS AND BARCALOUNGERS
- ☑ STIHL CHAIN SAWS
- ☑ PRESSURE WASHERS
- ☑ SUPER GLUE
- ☑ CORDLESS DRILLS
- ☑ WD-40
- ☑ DUCT TAPE
- ☑ SHOP VACS

Five hundred years ago, we would have lived in a house that we built ourselves with an axe. We would light a candle at the end of the day, make love to our wife (after all, we would have needed kids to help build a bigger house), and we'd be so damn tired that we'd fall asleep by eight. Now, with gadgets and tools to help us out, we have an easier life. It may be a life filled with more distractions, but being distracted is fun. So take off your tool belt, sit down, relax, and dive into a few of your favorite male distractions.

THE SWISS ARMY KNIFE

In 1891, Karl Elsener was making surgical tools when he discovered to his dismay that the Swiss army was carrying a pocket knife made in Germany. Was zur Hölle! In a fit of nationalistic pride he thought, "We can't have that," and designed the "soldier's tool" for the Swiss army. His original was made with a wood handle and contained a blade, a punch, a screwdriver, and a can opener. He named his company Victoria after his mother, and in 1921 the company became known as Victorinox when they added inox (a short version of the French word for stainless steel) to the knives.

In 1893, the Wenger Company also began making knives for the Swiss army, and in 1909, the Swiss government split the contract between the two companies to keep prices low. Splitting the orders also helped create jobs in two different parts of Switzerland (politics in the early 1900s). Victorinox advertised its knife as the Original Swiss Army Knife, while Wenger called its model the Genuine Swiss Army Knife. Victorinox bought Wenger in 2005 but still keeps both brands separate.

MAN-TASTIC FACT

In 2006, Wenger released a collectible novelty Swiss army knife called The Giant. It was over nine inches wide, contained eighty-seven tools, and sold for about $1,200.

The Swiss army knife gained fame—and its name—after World War II. U.S. GIs coming home from Europe brought home souvenirs that they had confiscated from German soldiers. The German soldiers were not issued the knives, but many bought them with their own money. GIs called the knife a "Swiss Officer's Knife" and they became a hit back home.

The Swiss army knife is still used by the Swiss army today, but more are sold as pocket knives and novelty items. Swiss army knives have even gone high tech now. Modern-day versions come with USB flash drives, laser pointers, MP3 players, and digital altimeters. Of course, you can still buy the low-tech version. You can even buy a mini version that doubles as a key ring. The Swiss army knife has even become part of pop culture.

Seinfeld paid homage to the illustrious knife by dedicating an entire episode to trying to figure out how the knife helped the Swiss win any wars. MacGyver escaped dozens of trouble spots with the help of his Swiss army knife and duct tape. (Give that man three minutes, a Swiss army knife, and duct tape and he could turn a tin can into a nuclear reactor.) The Museum of Modern Art even has one in its collection to show it as an art form. The venerable knife has also gone to the ends of the Earth (Everest and the poles) and has even gone to space with NASA astronauts. Hey, if this little tool of miniature mayhem is good enough for astronauts and for the defense of one of the richest countries in the world, it ought to be okay for us men.

TWO-IN-ONE SHAMPOO AND CONDITIONER

Men don't like to spend too much time grooming. We admit it. However, despite our impatience, we still want to look good (even though we may not always admit it). Fortunately, there is a product that suits all of our needs: 2-in-1 shampoo and conditioner.

The first 2-in-1 for men hit the market in 1987 (I remember because I still had hair in the 1980s), and Pert Plus was an instant success story. Now, a quick five-minute shower (real men don't take baths—at least not when we're alone) left us clean with good-looking hair. Within two years every shampoo maker on the planet had a 2-in-1 product available. And the number of good-looking men out there increased tenfold.

Luckily, baldness and buzz cuts have come into style for those who (like me) are challenged in the follicle department, but we still use a 2-in-1 on what little we have left. In fact, today, a few companies are even creating 3-in-1s that include shampoo, conditioner, *and* body wash. One bottle really can do it all.

MAN-DATE

In July 2009, Pert Plus teamed up with Six Flags Great America to attain a world record for a group shower. One hundred and fifty people showered in a custom-built, 40,000-square-foot outdoor shower. Bathing suits were required.

GAS-POWERED LEAF BLOWERS, SNOW BLOWERS, AND WEED WHACKERS

Falling leaves, knee-high weeds, and piles of snow have been around since the beginning of time, but we didn't really care until we began our flight to the suburbs. Then, the battle to win Yard of the Week began, and now men frantically try to out shovel, out rake, and out weed each other year round. Yes, we could achieve the same goals with push brooms, yard shears, and snow shovels, but where's the fun in that? Give us a fire-breathing gasoline-powered tool to do the same task and that yard work isn't as much of a chore.

The Japanese developed the first leaf blowers over a hundred years ago. These early blowers were hand-powered by a bellow, but did a suitable job of politely removing debris from tiny garden plots. But men yearned for more power so in the 1970s the Japanese added gas-powered engines. Now gas-powered leaf blowers are made by every power tool and lawn tool company under the sun (which you can see because all the damn leaves fell on my driveway). Gas-powered leaf blowers make short work of leaves and debris, and they make men feel pretty bad-ass. Who cares where the leaves go as long as they aren't littering up your

pretty driveway? The only problem with gas-powered leaf blowers? They're kind of addictive. The familiar hum of the blower can be heard virtually every morning in my neighborhood. Leaf blowing every day probably isn't that great for the environment because of the added exhaust, but let's be honest, men like being green but hate sweeping even more.

MAN-DATE

Steam-driven rotary snow blowers were developed in the 1800s to clear railroad tracks. The first practical street-driven snow blower was developed in 1925 by Arthur Sicard, a name still known for street snow-blowing. If you are really manly, you can still buy a road-ready blower from Sicard's company (now a division of SMI-Snowblast). Toro developed the first walk-behind snow blower in 1952.

Another marvel of yard work convenience is the weed whacker, also known as the string trimmer, garden trimmer, or Weed Eater (which is actually a brand name). George Ballas invented the weed whacker in 1971 after sitting in an automatic car wash. As the nylon bristles spun to clean his car, he had a "Eureka!" moment. The spinning brushes would be the perfect way to trim around his trees. He set out to make it happen. He grabbed a tin popcorn can from his trash and some nylon line, added a motor, and the Weed Eater company was born. The familiar whir of the spinning nylon has been a constant sound ever since. Just like with the leaf blower, you probably only fully appreciate this manvention if you've done yard work without one. Squeezing the old-fashioned gardening shears to trim was a pain in the ass. It would take an entire hour to do twenty feet of a chain link fence. With a weed whacker the work is done almost as fast as you can walk.

The snow blower is a manvention that men just love. Imagine, you're outside in a blizzard, determined to take back your driveway from the relentless flurries. A polite tug of the string, a shot from the adrenal gland, and you are off to launch snow back into the sky. Men don't really care where it falls as long as our driveways are clean. Well, we care a little. After all, it's pretty manly to clear off the driveway of our elderly next-door neighbors. After all, they bake us treats. And, as with most power tools, bigger is better. A five horsepower snow blower might work, but a ten horsepower two-stage Craftsman just looks more manly.

Gas-powered leaf blowers, snow blowers, and weed whackers are indispensable if you do your own yard work. These glorious, multiseason manventions have made lawn care less of a chore. Throw in a ride-on lawn mower and we're in man heaven.

AIR CONDITIONING

Air conditioning (AC) is one of man's little conveniences. Imagine driving a car on a summer day without it. Or watching the latest summer blockbuster dick flick in a theater with a broken AC. And, in addition to making the summer heat more bearable, AC also saves lives. Window screens, television, and AC, in addition to turning many men into couch potatoes, have all contributed to the eradication of most airborne mosquito diseases like malaria. Your choice seems to be malaria and certain death or a comfortable spot in the AC watching sports on the flat screen. I know which one I'd choose.

Crude forms of AC have been around for years. The Romans (at least the rich ones) built open channels in their homes through which they would circulate water. The wind blowing across the water cooled them down as their slaves fed them grapes. In Asia, people would hang grass mats in the windows. The grass mats were soaked in water and the water helped cool the air.

MAN-TASTIC FACT

Willis Carrier placed the first AC units in the White House, the Supreme Court, and the Capitol building. He also put the first AC in a sports arena when he installed a unit in Madison Square Garden.

Willis Carrier created the first modern AC in 1901. He designed an AC system to control the amount of heat and humidity in a printing plant in Brooklyn, New York; the printer's colored ink would not flow if the temperature and humidity reached a certain level. Carrier's unit used ammonia as the coolant, and it used spray nozzles to cool and dehumidify the air. These were large and expensive, but they got the job done.

Just as Carrier (and others) started to expand into the home market, the Great Depression and World War II intervened. Lack of money and a material shortage during the war caused AC sales to freeze until after the war. During the Great Depression, movie ticket sales boomed and AC helped. The movies offered cheap escapism and also a chance to bask in glorious cold air, since most theaters had AC units installed. After World War II, AC sales took off, and in 1953 alone, over one million AC window units were sold.

Can you even imagine living without AC now? Obviously, the amount of use yours gets depends on your location, but it sure is one manvention I wouldn't want to go without on a hot summer's day.

LA-Z-BOYS AND BARCALOUNGERS

When men get home from a hard day's work, we only want one thing: a comfortable place to rest our weary behinds. Enter the recliner, man's favorite resting place.

Cousins Edwin Shoemaker and Edward Knabusch created the first recliner in 1928 when they modified a wooden porch chair. The seat slid forward as the back reclined. Hence, the recliner was born, but they needed a name for it. The employees of the Floral City Furniture Company (the cousins' company) came to the rescue. La-Z-Boy won out over Sit-N-Snooze

MAN-DATE

In 2009, a Minnesota man was arrested for driving under the influence. What was he driving? You guessed it! A recliner. The police put the confiscated chair up for auction and it eventually sold for $3,700.

among others. Soon, dozens of companies joined in the man-needs-a-comfy-chair race and each took the recliner to new heights. (Barcalounger deserves special mention for adding the pop-up foot rest.)

Recliners morphed into "motion furniture" in the 1980s as interior design became more important than comfort. Fortunately, this manvention prevailed. Furniture designers hid recliners in the ends of couches, which concealed the reclining mechanism—and made our wives happy—but still allowed us men to put our feet up. Many of these same sofas also added flip-down console tables and cup holders. Newer recliners even add a flip-top armrest, which can hide a portable cooler, and a few even throw in an automatic massage feature—a double duty piece of manvention heaven.

STIHL CHAIN SAWS

Chain saws are a perfect manvention. They're loud. They're destructive. And what other tool can you use to both clear out an overgrown lot and kill video foes and gangsters?

The first chain saw designed to cut wood was a one-hundred-pound model patented by Andreas Stihl (a still respected name in chain saws) in 1926. This two-man electric beast was primarily

MAN-DATE

The first practical chain-driven saw wasn't designed for trees at all. It was designed for bone. In 1830, German physician Bernhard Heine developed the *osteotome*, a small hand-cranked chain saw used for cleaning the end of a bone, so Dr. Heine could have a clean mount for a prosthetic limb.

used only in sawmills and not in an actual forest. A few years later, Stihl created a gasoline-powered saw and cut the weight to a mere ninety pounds. After World War II, materials got lighter and stronger, and so did the one-man chain saw, which now weighed about forty sweat-inducing pounds. Today's chain saws weigh about ten pounds or so—and thank God they do. Can you imagine clearing brush or chasing after a zombie with a ninety pounder?

Another man who deserves a spot in the chain saw hall of fame is Oregon Saw Chain Company owner Joseph Cox, who revolutionized the chain on the chain saw in 1946. While cutting wood one day, he noticed timber beetle larva sawing through a tree and was inspired by the shape of the beetles' jaws to build a better chain saw. His updated chain, which included alternating metal C-shaped pieces, is still the type of chain used in most chain saws today.

MAN-DATE

In 1946, a Swiss engineer attached a saw blade to his wife's sewing machine and the jigsaw power tool was born.

Chain saws have also been adapted with concrete and metal cutting blades to broaden their appeal and make them a more specialized tool. Firemen and concrete workers love the convenience of wielding a chain saw to help with their jobs, and artists use chain saws to carve ice and tree trunks into amazing sculptures. In addition to felling trees and carving ice, chain saws have worked their way into pop culture. Haunted houses across the country are filled with chain saw–wielding maniacs. I mean, who can forget the *Texas Chainsaw Massacre* and all its variants? And anyone who has ever seen *Scarface* still cringes at the throaty sound of a chain saw. But whether you're wielding a chain saw for work, taking down a tree on your day off, or using a chain saw as a Halloween prop, this man tool is a first-class manvention.

PRESSURE WASHERS

In Chapter 7, we discussed the lust men have for the Super Soaker. But if men get that excited about a juiced-up squirt gun, imagine how we feel about the pressure washer. Holding that magic wand and pulling the trigger leads to two things: a flood of high-pressure, dirt-cutting water and an increase in adrenalin. Anything that streams water at more than 100 miles per hour and is too dangerous to point at your friends sounds like a pretty cool manvention to me.

The power washer came into existence during Prohibition—a dark era for men. Alcohol was outlawed, but many guys just didn't care and were resourceful enough to make their own. One of these men, Frank Ofeldt, was working in his garage on a homemade still for a friend of his when he noticed something amazing: the steam outlet of the still was shooting out a jet of water and steam that was cleaning the grease off his garage floor. The idea for the pressure washer was born. He joined forces with a few other men in the next few years to create his steam pressure washer. An aspiring ad man came in for an interview and asked what the device was going to be called. When Mr. Ofeldt said, "Hyperpressure Vapor Spray Generator," he quickly responded, "Why don't you call it the High Pressure Jenny?" The name stuck and the Jenny pressure washing company was born. Men have never looked back.

SUPER GLUE

Cracked plates. Shattered knickknacks. The broken handle on your favorite beer mug. Super Glue is a sure-fire way to mend anything, except for a broken heart. And actually doctors are now using Super Glue to mend people, so broken hearts may be fixed sooner than we realize. A manvention favorite, Super Glue sticks to everything, fingers included.

Super Glue belongs to a class of adhesives called *cyanoacrylates,* which were first discovered during World War II when engineers were looking for a way to make crystal clear gun sights. Cyanoacrylates are similar to a two-part epoxy. Mixing the two parts together causes the molecules to form long, straight-chained molecules with incredible strength. Working with these cyanoacrylates, those engineers soon developed this cool little glue that stuck to everything (at least anything with moisture on it). Unfortunately, this cool little glue was soon discarded because it stuck to literally *everything.*

In 1951, two researchers from the Eastman Kodak Company, Harry Coover and Fred Joyner, became determined to find a way to sell this glue. They discovered that moisture caused the cyanoacrylates to almost instantly form bonds and a few years later Eastman 910 was on the market (in air-tight bottles and tubes). The name was eventually changed to Super Glue. Different companies sell variations under names like Krazy Glue and Loctite.

MAN-DATE

Super Glue became a sensation in 1959 when Harry Coover appeared on the show *I've Got a Secret.* The host, Gary Moore, was lifted off the ground using two steel plates held together with only a single drop of Eastman 910 (now called Super Glue).

If you do happen to stick something together with Super Glue (like your fingers), there are ways to break the bond. As most people know, nail polish remover will soften cured Super Glue bonds due to the acetone in the product, which accounts for the wonderful smell. Another great way to unstick something that is stuck is dichloromethane, a fun chemical that is used in bubbling juke boxes, drinking birds, and hand boilers. Of course, dichloromethane is also used as a paint stripper, so it must be handled with care. Your body will also metabolize the chemical into carbon monoxide (which isn't so good for you). Ungluing your fingers is no good if you die in the process.

MAN-DATE

Harry Coover and Fred Joyner invented Super Glue in 1942. Thirty seconds later, man glued his fingers together for the first time.

Today, variations of Super Glue are even used by doctors to suture wounds. The medical super glue holds the wound together until it heals. Then the glue is shed from your body along with the dead skin. Using medical super glue in this way actually produces less scarring than using stitches or staples. In the 1980s we actually used store-bought Super Glue to close cuts on the rugby field. We would squeeze the cut together and put a drop on the outside to hold the flaps together. I would go to a professional now, but I was young and stupid.

As anyone who watches *CSI* knows, Super Glue also is great for finding latent fingerprints. Heat a little up (in a closed container), and the fumes bond with the amino acids left over in your fingerprint. The fumes

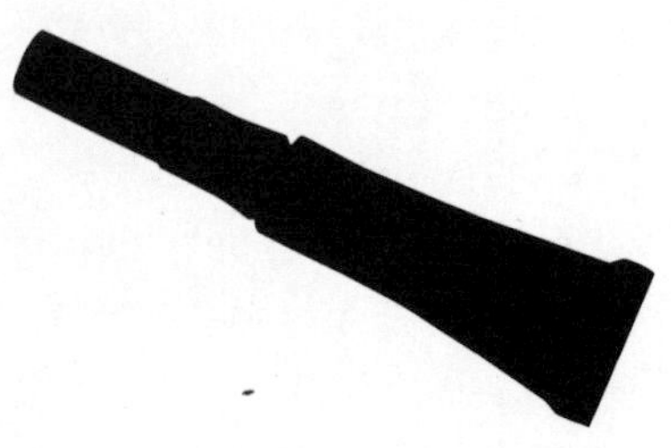

will also bond with any sweat or minute amounts of blood to further help the criminologist. You can now be a DIY detective. Just don't use this sweet manvention to glue yourself to a killer . . . .

CORDLESS DRILLS

Power and portability are two things that make men smile. After all, tools are much more fun without any strings attached. And this definitely applies to our next manvention: the cordless drill.

> **MAN-DATE**
>
> The most expensive cordless drill ever, the Apollo Lunar Surface Drill, removed sample cores from the moon in 1971. The drill also made it to the moon on Apollo 16 and 17.

Drills have undergone a huge makeover over the last, oh, several thousand years. They were developed about the first time a caveman needed to bore a hole in the end of his club for a lanyard. Electric drills were invented in the late 1800s as man mastered the electric motor, but the cords made them a pain in the ass. It's hard to work efficiently when you're tethered to your power source. Black & Decker actually made a cordless drill in 1961, but it never sold too well; the batteries they used didn't hold enough power to make them useful. The first mainstream cordless drills showed up in the early 1980s and featured rechargeable nickel cadmium batteries. These drills were portable and also gave you a workout cause the damn things were so heavy. Then came the lithium ion battery, which revolutionized the way men wield their equipment. Lithium ion batteries are rechargeable; they're also used in cell phones and iPods—which means today's drills are more affordable. They also hold more power than other batteries, so we can get through some pretty hard-core jobs easily. And really, it feels pretty good to harness that power—whether you're putting an addition onto your house or just building a beer pong table for your next party.

WD-40

What's blue and yellow and can fix what ails you? (As long as what ails you is squeaky hinges, stuck zippers, and hard-to-open windows.) A can of lubricating WD-40. The man can has earned its rightful spot on the manvention list for its thousands of uses, which, according to *www.wd40.com,* include getting gum out of carpet and tomato stains off of clothing. Finally there is something that will remove Chef Boyardee's orange sauce from clothes. WD-40 is also used to protect the Statue of Liberty. And if it's good enough for Lady Liberty, it is good enough for all of us. But one of my favorite

> **MAN-TASTIC FACT**
>
> **WD-40 has a fan club and offers up a new use for their product every day at their website, *www.wd40.com*.**

uses listed on the company's website is fishing. Seems a small spray on a lure will make fish just jump onto the hook. Imagine a depressed fisherman sitting in his boat when in desperation he grabs the blue-and-yellow can. Guess it really can work miracles . . . and it owes its start to a rocket scientist.

WD-40 was invented in a San Diego lab in 1953. Norm Larsen and the other two employees of the Rocket Chemical Company were looking for a rust-repellant and degreaser. Norm succeeded in his desired water displacement formula on the fortieth try and WD-40 was born. The makers of the Atlas missile bought the first commercial batch to prevent corrosion, but WD-40 gained a foothold in every man's world when employees took some home for their personal use. Norm experimented with putting WD-40 into aerosol form for the home market, and in 1958, WD-40 started its retail life. Men have never been happier.

MAN-DATE

In 1969, the Rocket Chemical Company changed its name to the WD-40 Company.

DUCT TAPE

Duct tape has earned its spot near the top of the manvention list for always being there when a quick fix was needed. A leaky muffler? Duct tape. A hole in Grampa's shoes? Duct tape. A cabinet door that won't stay closed? Duct tape. It's strong enough to pull a car but simple to tear. What else could a guy want?

Johnson and Johnson developed the tape in 1942 for the U.S. military to use to keep ammo crates watertight. It worked for that, but it did oh so much more. Soldiers used it for everything, and when they came home, they continued to demand the tape. The original name of the product was *duck* tape. Why? No one knows for sure, but water rolled off of it like water off a duck's back, and it is also made with cotton duck cloth, so maybe one of these factors came into play.

After World War II, duck tape's versatility allowed it to help with the suburban construction boom. Builders used it to seal air-conditioning ducts, and a new name was born: duct tape. Originally duct tape only came in one color: olive drab green, but after World War II a few new colors were also born, most notably silver. Today's duct tape comes in every color, and no man should ever be without a roll.

MAN-TASTIC FACT

Ductigami, the art of fashioning creations with duct tape, has reached new levels in the last twenty years. The Duck Brand Company sponsors a contest every year to the best dressed couples with prom outfits made entirely out of their tape. You can go to *www.duckbrand.com* and find the winners under Promotions. You will be amazed.

But what makes duct tape such a great manvention? The tape is composed of three layers. The bottom layer is a thick and sticky adhesive. The middle layer is the cotton duck cloth, and the outside is covered with the waterproof plastic. It owes its versatility to all three. The waterproofing is great. The tape sticks to anything. And the cotton duck cloth allows you to tear it across the grain but provides tons of strength along the long direction. Perfection!

SHOP VACS

Men will take anything with a little bit of power and lay claim to it. The shop vacuum is the perfect example. Vacuums were designed to alleviate the drudgery of housework—which is *not* a good manvention—but the shop vac took things to a whole other level. There is absolutely nothing wrong with using a manly vac that comes with enough horsepower to suck up everything in sight. And we owe it all to a horse-drawn behemoth from days gone by.

MAN-DATE

In 1938, more than 70 percent of all vacuum cleaners were sold door-to-door.

The first practical vacuum cleaner came from an Englishman named Hubert Cecil Booth, in 1901. Until then cleaning was done by blowing dirt around and hoping to catch it with a feather duster. Booth witnessed a mechanical aspirator blowing dust and his mind went to work. He immediately wondered if he could reverse the effect of the aspirator and suck up the dirt instead of spewing it out. At a restaurant a few days later he demonstrated his idea to his dinner guests. He used his mouth to suck on a handkerchief that he laid on the fabric chair and ended up with a handkerchief full of dirt. The discovery was a gold mine for Booth. The first vacuum, named the Puffing Billy, was patented later that year and soon became a common sight on London's roads. The horse-drawn device was so large that it couldn't fit through doors. It stayed outside while eighty-foot-long hoses did the cleaning. Just imagine a shop vac so big it needed to be pulled by a car . . . man heaven.

Portable vacs followed in the next few years and were perfect for housewives. But manly men longed for something more. Shop-Vac (the company) came to our rescue in 1953. They put the vacuum into the hands of man when they put a remarkable wet/dry vacuum on the market. Not only could we suck up sawdust and other manly things, but we could also suck up water! The motor in Shop-Vac's wet/dry vacuum is protected by a float that shuts the motor off if the water gets too high. Finally, a foolproof way to clean! Now if someone would just put a 3-horsepower motor on a toilet brush . . . .

The Top Ten Manliest Movies Ever

1. *300*
2. *Enter the Dragon*
3. *Animal House*
4. *Die Hard*
5. *Gladiator*
6. *Jaws*
7. *Blazing Saddles*
8. *Predator*
9. *Fight Club*
10. *The Godfather*

CHAPTER 9

Lingerie and Other Feminine Distractions:

Uncover the Secrets of the Fairer Sex

Inside This Chapter You Will Find:

- ☑ Thongs and G-Strings
- ☑ Playboy Magazine
- ☑ Viagra
- ☑ String Bikinis
- ☑ The Sports Illustrated Swimsuit Issue
- ☑ Breast Implants
- ☑ The Tramp Stamp
- ☑ Condoms
- ☑ Free Porn
- ☑ Birth Control Pills

Women frustrate and confuse us, but they also make us happy. They're one of life's little mysteries. The feminine form has long been considered an art form, and more paintings, pictures, and sculptures have been done of women than any other topic. Who are we to argue with art? Men love the look, smell, and feel of the feminine body, and the things associated with women are some of mankind's great manventions. So put down that Victoria's Secret catalog and let's take a look.

THONGS AND G-STRINGS

Men love a tiny bit of mystery with a promise of more to come, and thongs and G-strings give us both. What's the difference between these two delicious manventions? After hours of exhaustive research and thumbing through ten years' worth of Victoria's Secret catalogs, the realization dawned that all G-strings are thongs but not all thongs are G-strings. A G-string (sometimes called T-backs by nonstrippers) is one tiny triangle in the front and a lot of string in the back. A thong has two triangles, one larger one for the front and a smaller one for the top crack of the ass. Either way, men love them (at least on the right ass).

These tiny pieces of fabric made their first public appearance in 1939. New York mayor Fiorello LaGuardia (he of the airport fame) wanted to show the best side of the Big Apple when it hosted the World's Fair. He mandated that all nude dancers cover themselves, and the thongs did the job (but just barely). The thong caught on in adult circles in the United States, but it wasn't very popular with people who made their living with clothes on until later—except in uninhibited Europe and South America where butt floss reigned (and still reigns) supreme.

MAN-DATE

Fashion designer Rudi Gernreich was credited with introducing the first modern thong-back bathing suit in 1974.

Thongs and G-strings have became popular in the United States in the last twenty years because women were looking for a way to wear underwear without putting their panty lines front and center. Men don't really care about panty lines, but we sure do love the solution. Thank you Mayor LaGuardia.

PLAYBOY MAGAZINE

Hugh Hefner started *Playboy* magazine in his kitchen in Chicago, in 1953. He decided that men needed female nudity in a high-class package, and he worked hard to make his—and our—dreams come true. Frankly, he wasn't sure how well the magazine would sell—the first issue didn't even have a date on the cover—but sell it did. From this small beginning, this manvention grew to be the most popular men's magazine in the world.

Hefner actually wasn't going to call the magazine *Playboy* at all. He was going to call it *Stag Party*,

MAN-TASTIC FACT

Although she appeared in the first issue (December 1953), Marilyn Monroe was never a Playmate and she never even posed for *Playboy* magazine. The picture used in the issue was taken for a calendar, and in the magazine she was a called the "Sweetheart of the Month." Playmates began in January 1954.

but an outdoor magazine called *Stag* threatened to sue for trademark infringement and the name was changed. One of *Playboy's* cofounders, Eldon Sellers, suggested naming the magazine after the Playboy Motor Company, where his mom had worked as a secretary. Playboy Motors may have only produced ninety-seven cars in its lifetime, but the name has lived on in the pantheon of maleness. And after all, naked women get men's engines running, so naming the magazine after a car company made sense.

Hefner pissed off a lot of prudish people with his magazine, but over the years it became accepted in journalistic circles. Jimmy Carter, Malcolm X, Steve Jobs, Fidel Castro, and Martin Luther King, Jr. have all been interviewed on the pages of *Playboy,* and Kurt Vonnegut, Arthur C. Clarke, John Steinbeck, and Ernest Hemingway have all graced the pages with their writing. *Playboy* has also created controversy with a few of their ideas. No college president wants to see his school at the top of *Playboy's* top party school list, and, having girls featured in issues doesn't bring whoops of joy from the president's office, either. The Big Ten, SEC, and even Conference USA have all seen coeds get naked for *Playboy.*

Playboy peaked in the 1970s and has begun a slow slide since then. The magazine only publishes ten issues a year now, which is too bad for chiropractors. *Playboy* has probably led to thousands of back injuries

MAN-DATE

Since 1970, *Playboy* has been produced in Braille. I guess some people really do read it for the articles.

for both women *and* men. Let's face it, most of us hid our copies beneath the mattress in our youth, and sleeping on a tilted mattress in your teen years can't be good for your back. But the pain was well worth it.

VIAGRA

It's a sad fact of life. As men age, it's likely that we'll get less wood, which is a bummer. Fortunately, erectile dysfunction (ED) medications are here to save the day. They are heavily advertised, heavily sold, and heavily joked about, and the king of the ED meds is Viagra—and for some men, it's a favorite manvention.

ED meds owe their beginning to one of the most attention-grabbing conference talks of all time. In 1983, the American Urological Association asked British researcher Dr. Giles Brindley to give a presentation on his research into erectile dysfunction at their convention in Las Vegas. People had assumed impotence was driven by the brain, but Brindley's attention-grabbing presentation changed all of that. Taking the stage in front of approximately eighty people wearing ill-fitted sweat pants, he gave an account of research that involved injecting his own Mr. Happy with drugs to produce an erection. After explaining that no person would find giving an academic science talk to be erotic, he stated that he had injected himself with papaverine in his hotel room before the lecture. He dropped trou to show the world his source of happiness. Mr. Happy stood at attention for all of the

MAN-DATE

In 1983, one of the best attention-grabbing lectures leads to a cure for impotence. Thankfully, what happens in Vegas doesn't always stay in Vegas.

guests to see. Brindley even waddled into the audience to have guests make sure it wasn't a trick. He pulled up his pants after everybody in the room stopped breathing. Dr. Brindley had proved to everyone that impotence was a physiological reaction and not just a psychological one. The race was on to find a cure for impotence, and within a few years, drugs had been found that would allow the Big Kahuna to surf any wave at any time.

Viagra was actually designed to treat high blood pressure and angina, but something "popped up" during the clinical trials. (Guess nothing treats high blood pressure like a hard on.) And giving guys their dream makers back is far more lucrative than angina and blood pressure medication. Today, the little blue prescription for love is the best-known drug in the world.

STRING BIKINIS

The bikini created a stir with its introduction that still hasn't died down. Two French designers simultaneously created the modern bikini in 1946. Jacques Heim sold his tiny two-piece swimsuits in Cannes on the French Riviera. He named his suit the Atome after the smallest particle of matter known at the time, the atom, and hired skywriters to advertise the Atome over the beach. Another designer, Louis Reard, created a similar suit and called his the bikini. Three weeks after Heim, he hired skywriters to write "Bikini: smaller than the smallest bathing suit in the world." Reard's name stuck, and the bikini is still a favorite manvention today.

MAN-DATE

In 1994, the bikini was designated as the official uniform for the sport of beach volleyball in the Olympics.

The bikini was named after Bikini Atoll, where the United States was doing nuclear bomb testing. Reard thought his creation would create as much shock as the atomic bomb, and he was right. He couldn't even find a supermodel to wear the suit, so he hired nude dancer Micheline Bernardini as his model. She liked the fact that she actually got to cover up and work for once. The bikini slowly became a hit.

The funny thing is that two-piece bathing suits were not new. Fourth-century mosaics found in Sicily show women wearing bathing suits similar to modern-day bikinis, and statues of Venus wearing two-piece bikini-like outfits have been found in the ruins of Pompeii. Reard's and Heim's bathing suits were just skimpier and actually had the nerve to expose the navel. The horror of it all!

MAN-TASTIC FACT

National health plans in Holland, Sweden, and much of Europe subsidize boob jobs.

Today, the king of the bikini is the string bikini, which

sun-worshipping women love almost as much as men. Exported from the beaches of Brazil in the 1970s, the string bikini took the world by storm. Maximizing sun exposure and moving the string leaves virtually no tan line on the side, which everyone agrees is a pretty great thing. Thank god for the French and their tiny pieces of fabric. Viva la France.

THE *SPORTS ILLUSTRATED* SWIMSUIT ISSUE

Combining sports and gorgeous women seems to be standard nowadays, but that wasn't always the case. The *Sports Illustrated* swimsuit issue helped to put the two on a collision course. The magazine also helped define the term *supermodel* and, for all those doubters out there, proved the old adage that sex sells. Today, the magazine is one of the top-selling magazines in the world yearly.

The *Sports Illustrated* swimsuit issue made its debut in 1964. The editor, Andre Laguerre, was looking for a topic to cover during the slow winter months. And boy, did he hit the nail on the head. What guy wouldn't want to look at pictures of beautiful women, especially during the winter when the majority of ladies are covered up. Laguerre enlisted a relatively unknown, Jule Campbell, to help him with the shoot and the pictures. She is now a superstar in the modeling world, and the cover of the swimsuit edition is one of the most desired slots in the world.

Nothing creates a buzz like controversy, and the swimsuit issue had controversy in spades. The outrage over the magazine made it a sensation. Yearly, parents, wives, and librarians show contempt for this particular issue. *SI* even makes a bigger deal of it by printing letters from outraged subscribers two weeks after the issue drops. The magazine continued to get racier every year until they hit the point of no return. In 1978, Cheryl Tiegs posed for a shot wearing a white fishnet bathing suit. The top was opaque until it got wet; then it was translucent. The issue was an instant hit and created a large controversy. It also helped SI because now anything they print short of full nudity is okay compared to Cheryl's nipples peeking through.

The names of the swimsuit issue cover girls are permanently engraved on the male psyche: Bar, Heidi, Cheryl, Kathy, Brooklyn, and Marissa. And every February, we men rush to the mailbox to celebrate the feminine form. A bonus is that the magazine actually has some sports stuff in it. And sports + nearly naked women = a manvention made in heaven.

MAN-DATE

In 1975, a relatively unknown model named Christie Brinkley debuted a string bikini in the *Sports Illustrated* swimsuit issue. Due to this exposure, she became one of the top supermodels in the world.

BREAST IMPLANTS

Men love tatas. We love them big, round, and perky. But for women past the age of twenty, big, round, and perky breasts often mean surgery. Guys have their preferences, but the majority vote yes for boob jobs. And why not? We love the cleavage in the summer and the tight sweaters in the winter, and boob jobs just help a poor girl fill out her clothes a little better.

The first breast augmentation procedures were attempted in the 1890s when doctors would inject paraffin (wax) directly into the bazookas to make them bigger. This was the preferred method for about thirty years, but it was eventually replaced when doctors realized they could just take fat from a chick's ass and inject it into her boobs, causing them to grow. Silicone first came into play in the 1960s, but it wasn't initially used as an implant. Doctors just injected silicone directly into the boobs until they reached the desired cup size. Imagine taking a tube of caulk and helping your lady friend out. It didn't work, and it caused severe health problems. A few doctors even tried sponges, all in the search for larger fun bags.

In today's world, implants come in two varieties: silicone implants that are commonly called "gummy bear" types because of their consistency (you may never look at gummy bears the same), and saline (salt water) implants. But no matter the type, men love them. We love them at the beach, on the silver screen, at the mall, at our favorite gentleman's club . . .

THE TRAMP STAMP

For years, tattoos were confined to sailors, convicts, Polynesians, and long-haul truck drivers, but in the last twenty years tats have reached the mainstream. More and more, tattoos are seen as an expression of personal style and taste—and rebellion. Men see a woman with ink and no longer wonder what prison she was in. Instead, we wonder how we can get in touch with that wild side.

A cute butterfly on the ankle suggests that a woman is sensitive (and a little daring). Barbed wire around the arm scares most men, but it also makes us wonder. But the king of get-your-motor-running tats is the lower back tat. Lovingly called a "tramp stamp" by most men, the lower back tat is a huge turn-on. There's nothing like finding out that the cute, innocent-looking redhead at the bar has a secret rebellious side.

Many women actually get their tattoos on their lower backs because it's convenient. The back provides a large flat canvas for the artist and won't stretch as much later in life. It is also easy to hide at the office. Honestly though, men don't care about the reasons why a woman decided to get a tramp stamp. We only care that there's one there. Because if there's a tat on a chick's lower back, who knows what else we'll find when we get her home?

MAN-DATE

In 2009, Mattel released a Barbie doll with ink across the lower back. Bet Ken was pumped.

CONDOMS

No glove, no love. Never take a shower without a raincoat. Don't go sliding unless your penis is hiding. We've heard them all. Condoms are a wonderful manvention that lets us go swimming in potentially shark-infested waters. Single men, don't leave home without one (or a few). Today, we have flavored condoms, glow-in-the-dark condoms, studded condoms, and ribbed condoms. Throughout history a variety of condoms have been available, but some are a little scary.

History has swallowed up the tale of the original condom inventor, and we're not even sure how the word *condom* came into being, although the best guess is it comes from the word *condos*, Latin for "receptacle." When it comes right down to it, men are just extremely glad they were invented. Condom materials have changed over the years, but a good many earlier models focused on animal parts; bladders and intestines were commonly used. The Chinese used paper (which may account for why there are over a billion Chinese), and the Japanese are reported to have used either leather or tortoise shells. In the mid-1800s, most civilizations settled on rubber (there's nothing like a car tire on your dick). Luckily, latex soon became the choice for men because it was thinner than the other options, didn't have

MAN-TASTIC FACT

Edible condoms are available, just don't go swimming with these on. They are a novelty only. They will not prevent little ones or diseases.

MAN-DATE

Many people think that syphilis lead to the death of Napoleon Bonaparte in 1821. He had high levels of arsenic in his blood, which was a common treatment for syphilis at the time. Guess the treatment really is worse than the disease.

a smell, and could be molded into any shape and dyed any color. The modern condom was born.

Condoms were socially unacceptable to many men for years, but luckily that has changed. A hundred years ago, you swam without a suit and got your choice of a few diseases that could be cured with a shot. Nowadays, you can get diseases that you keep forever, and condoms keep everything on the up and up. And besides, glow-in-the-dark condoms are fun, especially if you want to keep track of your bits and pieces in a blackout.

FREE PORN

Men have always loved porn. From cabaret to peep shows to porno mags, we've found lots of ways to get our fix. Fortunately, today, we don't even have to leave the house to get off, and we can find anything we're interested in on the Internet. And the best thing about it is it's free.

Just imagine the days before Internet porn. Men had to go to a porn theater to see moving, moaning, naked women—and there is nothing sexy about thirty men collectively waxing their johnsons at the same time. Or you had to stroll into an adult bookstore after hiding your car around the corner. Today's men no longer have to deal with these indignities. We have been liberated. Now all you have to do is wait until you are alone and log on.

Porn is also responsible for pop-up blockers, the program that keeps extra pages of ads from opening on your computer. In the early days of computer porn (like the 1990s), a venture to a porn site turned your computer into an epileptic-fit-inducing series of pop-up ads. After you finished with your seizure, you turned the computer off just to stop them. Pop-up blockers were designed to save us from this. With pop-up blockers and firewalls, we are able to surf away. And what guy doesn't like an uninterrupted good time?

MAN-TASTIC FACT

Only female mosquitoes bite. Male mosquitoes are only there to service the females.

BIRTH CONTROL PILLS

MAN-DATE

Who you gonna call? Ron "The Hedgehog" Jeremy, one of the top male porn stars of all time, was an extra for the movie *Ghostbusters* in 1984.

Every man has his own personal preference when it comes to sex. Some love being tender and making love for hours. Some like it quick and dirty. But no man wants to spend the next month worrying about an unplanned baby. Enter "the Pill": the form of birth control that gave men the freedom to do their business without worrying.

The earliest form of birth control was coitus interruptus, and it's the "interruptus" part that most men have problems with. Some things should not be interrupted. Along came condoms, which were safe (and prevented most diseases), but they just don't feel as good as the real thing. When we're in a committed relationship, we want to go swimming without a suit. The Pill was developed in the 1950s and came to the United States in 1960. Finally men could get down to the business without worry. And the best part? When the Pill is involved, guys don't really have to do anything at all except enjoy the moment. No pulling out. No stopping to put on a condom. We're in. We're out. And we do it all with peace of mind.

MAN-TASTIC FACT

It is a myth that women absolutely cannot get pregnant during a visit from the "Red Tide."

Birth control pills work by tricking the woman's body into thinking she is already pregnant. If she is pregnant, there's no need for her body to shoot an egg down her fallopian tube. And if there's no egg, your swimmers just swim around a while and die—alone. I don't know any guy who wouldn't trade a few thousand swimmers for a worry-free mattress marathon.

The Top Ten Most Useless Manventions of All Time

1. Electric pizza cutter
2. Reality TV
3. Remote control fart machines
4. Electric bicycles
5. Cordless jump ropes
6. All-terrain office chairs
7. Fish 'n Flush
8. Gerbil shirt
9. Outfits for your dog
10. Motorized ice cream cones

CHAPTER 10

Wheels and More:

GENTLEMEN, REV YOUR ENGINES

INSIDE THIS CHAPTER YOU WILL FIND:

- ☑ The Terrafugia Flying Car
- ☑ The Prius
- ☑ NASCAR
- ☑ Cruise Control
- ☑ Riding Lawn Mowers
- ☑ TomToms and Garmins
- ☑ Harley-Davidson
- ☑ The Can-Am Renegade
- ☑ Pickup Trucks
- ☑ Bumper Nuts

Ever since their invention, men have been obsessed with cars. For guys, what we drive is usually a status symbol, and hard-core muscle cars, motorcycles, and pickup trucks all make us feel pretty good about ourselves. Today's vehicles also come pimped out with things that make our lives easier and make us look smarter, like cruise control and GPS navigation (finally, we no longer have to ask for directions!). So put it in park and let's examine the world of rolling manventions.

THE TERRAFUGIA FLYING CAR

Mermaids. Sasquatch. Cars that fly. Do they actually exist? Are they just myths? Well, who has any idea if mermaids or Bigfoot are real; cryptozoologists have been hunting them down for centuries. But, as far as the flying car is concerned, it sure is real—even if it's not on the street (in the air?). If you hate traffic jams, this is the car for you. No guy likes sitting in bumper-to-bumper traffic, and this plane/car is perfect for us impatient, traffic-hating men.

> **MAN-DATE**
>
> The Aerocar was created by Moulton Taylor in 1949. He produced six prototypes but never made a commercial product.

The Terrafugia Transition is a two-seat airplane that drives on the road. (Check it out at *www.terrafugia.com*.) It is a funny-looking car, so you will get some stares, but being able to fly over stalled interstates is a trade any man would take. And besides, most of the stares are just stares of envy. Imagine, you wake up in the morning, back the Transition out of the garage, fold down the wings, and rev up the engine to fly to work. When you get close to the office, just land, press a button to fold in the wings, and finish your drive. Like all male toys worth having, it takes a few coins to own one, but just knowing that someday mankind will be able to fly their asses to work is enough for me.

THE PRIUS

Guys love green; both the cold, hard cash variety and the stuff that makes us environmentally responsible. Our next manvention, the Prius, helps us on both counts. It tells the ladies that we have a sensitive side, but it also saves us some cold, hard cash by getting almost 50 miles per gallon. So we get admiration from the ladies, extra green in our wallet, and a greener Earth. Sounds like a win, win, win situation to me.

The Toyota Prius is the king of the hybrid cars, but it's not the only one. Almost every car manufacturer offers its own hybrid. Green sells. Hybrids use a combination of an electric motor, batteries, and a good old gasoline engine. The gas engine creates energy to power the car and charge the batteries, but the electric motor is the key to most hybrids. Electricity takes over (and the gas engine shuts off) when there is enough juice in the battery. And if the gas engine isn't running, obviously no gas is burned. It sounds so good that you can't help but wonder why we weren't able to come up with something like this before. Well, hybrid cars are not as new as most people think.

MAN-DATE

In 1807, a Swiss by the name of François Isaac de Rivaz invented the first internal combustion engine. It actually burned hydrogen (with outside oxygen) to create power. The cars that ran on this "water engine" stored hydrogen gas in a balloon attached to the car.

Almost all of the early cars were electric, but they had limited range (less than twenty miles). Ford added a gas engine in 1896 to increase the range, and gas engines ruled for the next 100 years. But the Prius was an instant hit when it was introduced in Japan in 1998, and sales have exploded in the United States since it was introduced here in 2000. Which makes Mother Nature—and us men—very happy drivers.

NASCAR

We've already discussed the fact that men like fast cars, women, and booze. And nothing could be better than a sport that combines all three. So, thank God for NASCAR (National Association of Stock Car Racing).

NASCAR was born in the 1920s and 1930s in the South, the land of moonshine. And if you are going to "run shine," you need a fast car, so shine runners would take a stock car like an ugly Chevy and have a little fun. When you're trying to get somewhere fast, you need speed, and anything goes in the engine department. You also want to lighten the load so you can outrun the cops. It also has to look like every other ugly ass Chevy in town. It does no good to run shine at night if Johnny Law is going to

> ***MAN-TASTIC FACT***
>
> The term *bootlegger* comes from the Old West. It was illegal to sell booze to the Native Americans. Intrepid cowboys would smuggle in flasks of illegal booze in their boots.

MAN-DATE

In 1907, Billy Durant, the founder of General Motors, found the now-familiar bow-tie logo for Chevrolet on wallpaper in a Paris hotel room. He tore off a piece, stuck it in his wallet, and brought it back to Detroit. Louis Chevrolet, a French racecar driver, joined with Durant to start Chevrolet. Durant pulled out the logo as they worked. Louis Chevrolet left the company shortly afterwards, and Chevy was rolled into General Motors in 1915. The name and logo survived.

recognize the car tomorrow in the Wal-Mart parking lot.

While bootleggers were racing the cops in the rural South, a beach in Florida became the ultimate speed hangout: Daytona Beach. The Daytona Beach race course (half the course was actually on the beach!) was the top place in the world for racers in the 1920s and 1930s. Men flocked to see these souped-up cars do battle. And it didn't take long for the shine runners to get involved. The two worlds collided when Bill France Sr. decided that racers needed to be protected from unscrupulous promoters. He thought people would enjoy watching normal cars haul ass (and wreck), and in 1947 NASCAR was founded to the delight of country boys everywhere.

Out of that humble beach and booze beginning came the second-most-watched sport in the United States (football is king). Most tracks seat over a hundred thousand soon-to-be-sun-baked fans and each televised race is good for another ten million or so fans (at least according to NASCAR). Fans spend more than

$3 billion each year on licensed NASCAR apparel (and maybe even more on counterfeit flea market stuff). And NASCAR brings us women, both in the stands, sports bars, and victory lane where a bevy of beauties are there to help the driver celebrate. But most of us wouldn't watch if it wasn't for the crashes. Cars spinning out of control at 200 miles per hour make the hours of watching left-hand turns worth it.

CRUISE CONTROL

Most of the time men are the ones who end up driving. Why? Who knows, but we just automatically go around to the driver's side and get in. We don't mind. We love to drive, and driving is easier today because of cruise control. If you're going to be driving at the same speed for a while (like on the highway), all you have to do is set it and forget it. You still have to pay attention to where you're going and if you need to slow down, but you don't have to worry about being pulled over because you somehow accelerated your Porsche up to 100 miles per hour without realizing.

The inventor of cruise control was actually blind, but don't worry,

MAN-TASTIC FACT

Manhole covers are round for a reason. Round covers can never fall down the manhole regardless of how they are turned. Virtually every other shape could be turned where it could fall down the hole.

he never got behind the wheel. Ralph Teetor was an engineer and a prolific inventor. Almost all of his patents dealt with cars, but cruise control is his most famous. One day, Ralph was driving with his lawyer. His lawyer slowed down while talking and sped up while listening. This herky-jerky ride got Ralph's wheels turning and the idea for cruise control was born. He was determined to create a speed control device.

MAN-DATE

The 1958 Chrysler Imperial not only came with cruise control, but it also featured electric door locks and a push-button transmission.

Ralph spent the next few years tinkering and was finally awarded a patent in 1945. But it took more than ten years to perfect this idea. Finally, in 1958, cruise control was ready for the men of the world. Chrysler's New Yorker, Imperial, and Windsor all featured cruise control, although it was a few years before that name was adopted. Early on, cruise control was given names like Speedostat, Controlomatic, Touchomatic, and Pressomatic. But the considered name that scares the hell out of me is Auto Pilot.

Cruise control works when a speed sensor from the wheels sends a signal to the throttle to change the engine rpms to keep you at the same speed. The car maintains the speed by the use of a vacuum or solenoid-driven throttle cable. Cruise control will disengage when you touch the brake or the clutch. Most cars allow you to press the gas without disengaging; when you release the gas you will go back to the cruise speed.

Most car companies are working with adaptive cruise control for the next generation of cars. These adaptive units will add radar to the mix. The car will use radar to judge how far the next car is in front of you, and your speed will then be adjusted to keep a safe following distance. And if the radar works to the front, how long will it be until they develop radar that works in all directions? Then we could incorporate the steering wheel and truly have autopilot. Scary idea, but if it works, it would be a great manvention.

MAN-TASTIC FACT

Police lights are blue while other emergency vehicles have red lights. Years ago, police cars had red lights. Drivers would claim they sped up because they were trying to get out of the way of emergency vehicles. The police changed to a more visible color to eliminate that alibi.

RIDING LAWN MOWERS

Mowing the yard is usually a chore that men do grudgingly, but riding lawn mowers changed all that. Now men can just hop on the mower and feel pretty badass as we cut the grass. You get outside to smell cut grass, you get the yard mowed, and you get to drive a large piece of heavy machinery around on your property. Sounds like a pretty awesome manvention—especially if you live in the suburbs.

Riding mowers got their start in the sports world, and several horse-pulled and steam-driven versions were available in the 1800s. These early mowers were designed to mow polo, cricket, and soccer fields. Most used a reel-type mower, which is still the preferred type for sports stadiums. Reel mowers use one set of revolving blades to cut the grass as it comes in contact with a stationary blade (called a bed knife or bed blade). But it took rotary power and the move away from agriculture to get us common folk mowing yards.

MAN-DATE

John Deere died in 1886, long before his company ever sold a riding lawn mower (or even a green-and-yellow tractor). John started his company by making steel plows in the 1830s.

In the early 1900s, rotary mowers were born when several people independently mounted saw blades to small gas-powered motors. Variations of these tools continued to be improved upon, but it took suburban bragging rights to really up the ante. The move to suburbs after WWII changed all that, and home riding lawn mowers added to the competition. Larger yards needed more power than a manual reel mower could deliver. And besides, no man wanted to spend eight hours cutting the grass when more power was available. Now men could have good-looking lawns and have the joy of gasoline-powered motion at the same time. In 1973, the go-kart/lawn mower connection got a great boost in a pub in England. (It is amazing how a little lubrication may start the brain thinking.) These blokes were lamenting the high cost of auto racing. One of them suggested lawn mower racing, and the British Lawn Mower Association was formed. The sport is fun to watch and cheap to do. Just take an ordinary riding mower (you are not allowed to modify the engine) and away you go.

Give a man a riding lawn mower and the yard is no longer a chore but a way to race, and anything that can make yard work fun is a great manvention as far as men all over the world are concerned.

TOMTOMS AND GARMINS

Men hate to ask for directions. We will drive the roads for hours to avoid asking for help, but luckily we never have to ask again, thanks to the tiny computer screen (and the mysterious, hot voice) on the global positioning system (GPS) unit in our cars. We men are a simple lot. We prefer being told what to do, and many of us would do anything for a girl who sounds hot. And if we're told to take a left in 500 feet, you'd better believe that we're taking that left.

GPS was developed for the military to be able to track our troops (and launch missiles). First conceived in 1973, GPS first went to work in 1980 (but only for uniformed fighting men). In

1983, GPS was freed for the masses in response to the Russians shooting down a Korean airliner that wandered into their space. After the incident President Reagan ordered the military to open up its GPS system for civilian use so that commercial airliners will always know their location and won't wander into the wrong air space. The GPS system in use today features twenty-four satellites (plus a few more backups) to tell you exactly where you are. Your receiver, that TomTom or Garmin unit affixed to your dashboard, receives a signal from at least four of those satellites that tells the receiver how far away it is from each of the satellites. The receiver uses that information to compute your actual place on the Earth to within a couple of meters. That information is overlaid on a preprogrammed map so you can visualize your location.

Of course, most of the time men actually know how to get where they're going without a GPS, but it sure helps—and it keeps our wives and girlfriends off our ass when we're behind the wheel. Never again will we be forced to

MAN-DATE

The man responsible for many of our traffic laws, William Eno, never drove a car in his life. In 1903, he developed the first traffic code for New York City, and he later developed the traffic plans for Paris and London. He also invented stop signs, one-way streets, taxi stands, and the traffic circle, but he thought cars were a fad and never learned how to drive. At least he was wealthy enough to afford a chauffeur when he realized he was wrong.

stop for directions. It's so great that we even let the ladies use it, even if it's just to make the roads a safer place for all concerned.

HARLEY-DAVIDSON

Motorcycles are a definite guy favorite. Even those who don't ride still enjoy the sights and sounds of the throaty roar of a bike. We also secretly drool over the women who are straddling the back of a bike as we drive by in our air-conditioned minivan. There are lots of motorcycle makers out there now, but the undisputed king is and always will be Harley-Davidson. Let's take a look at how motorcycles were discovered before we ride off on a hog into the future of motorcycles.

The earliest recognizable motorcycle is the Roper Steam Velocipede. Sylvester Roper mounted a steam boiler on a "safety bicycle" and away he went. Safety bicycles are similar to the bikes that we ride today; they have two wheels that are usually the same size

MAN-DATE

GIs returned from World War II and started modifying their motorcycles. These "bikers" hung out in groups and originally called their bikes "bobbers." Thankfully that name was replaced by choppers. They chopped the tubes to lower the rear seat and chopped any extra accessories. In 1969, the movie *Easy Rider* brought the chopper into the public eye, and they have never left.

and handle bars to steer. Roper's steam-powered bike worked like a charm but didn't sell well. The concept of a super-hot boiler between a guy's legs was just not popular. It took a car pioneer, a carpenter, and a better engine to bring the next motorcycle to life.

In 1885, Gottlieb Daimler (of future Daimler-Benz fame) mounted an Otto engine on a wooden safety cycle. The Otto engine is one of the earliest internal combustion engines and is very similar to our car engines today. Daimler's motorcycle was made almost completely out of wood, but it had another feature that today's motorcycles don't. Attached to the bottom of the frame were two smaller wheels (kind of like training wheels) along with the two larger wheels. It is no wonder that Daimler quickly graduated to four-wheel automobiles.

In 1903, William Harley and the Davidson brothers built and sold their first motorcycle, which was designed for racing. In 1909, Harley-Davidson made the first motorcycle powered by a V-twin engine. It generated a whopping 7 horsepower. (Most of today's motorcycles can deliver over 100 horsepower.) Before long, Harley-Davidson (H-D) became the gold standard for manly bikes. H-Ds were loud, fast, and cool looking, and the fact that they make a lot of noise (enough to annoy your neighbors if you own one) is something H-D owners count as a bonus feature. Many H-D riders will tell you that "loud pipes save lives," because it lets

everybody know you are around. Loud pipes also scream "look at me," which is one of the reasons to buy a hard-core bike in the first place; after all, motorcycles are meant to be admired. Over the years, H-D has created some of the most coveted motorcycles ever designed—the Knucklehead, the Flathead, the Panhead, the Shovelhead, the Fat Boy, and the Softail—and they remain king of the road today. Even if there is a little more competition now.

After World War II, the Japanese got into the motorcycle game. These derogatively named "rice-burners" were cheap, attractive, reliable, and powerful. Honda, Kawasaki, and Yamaha began to dominate the field in the 1960s, and these bikes had an electric start, which meant no more kick-starting. The Japanese were also the first to make your junk tingle with a motorcycle. Sport bikes exploded in the 1980s because of their speed and ability to do stunts. These "crotch rockets" were fast and agile. Typically, cruiser-style bikes may be more popular for the older set, but crotch rockets rule the young set. If you're over thirty-five, you are going for a Sunday ride on a comfortable cruiser. If you're under thirty-five, you are

MAN-DATE

In 1896, seventy-two-year-old Sylvester Roper took his steam motorcycle to the Charles River bicycle race track in Boston to demonstrate the ability of his bike to set a pace for the racing bicycles. After a few laps, the riders cleared the track to watch Roper race the steam bike. After a few laps, the bike started to wobble and crashed. Roper was dead on impact (although he actually died of heart failure).

MAN-DATE

James Dean loved his Porsche Spyder. After the crash that took his life, the legendary George Barris bought the car. Barris was the creator of the original 1960s Batmobile, the Monkeemobile, and the Beverly Hillbillies' truck. The Porsche wreck toured the United States to promote driving safety. The car wreck disappeared in 1960 and has never been seen since. The wreck is worth a million dollars if you can find it.

going to make your crotch tingle as you head out to the club, pop a few wheelies and nose stands, and have a great night.

It's important to mention that scooters are not a motorcycle or a manvention. They are only cool if you deliver pizzas in New York City or are zipping around on the back roads of Southern California. So don't make a mistake and think you're hard core if you bought your bike in pastel.

THE CAN-AM RENEGADE

In 1967, U.S. Honda dealers asked their parent company to figure out something they could sell in the winter when motorcycle sales were thin. The company agreed, and Honda started work on a manvention that would lead millions of men to get dirty and love it. In 1969, Honda released the US90 ATV, which ran at a whopping 7 horsepower. Compared to today's ATVs that run somewhere between 40 to 100 horsepower, the US90 was pretty disappointing. The ATVs didn't have any suspension, but it did come with comically large balloon-like tires to soften the jarring feeling on your ass as you went off-road. Most of the major Japanese motorcycle companies soon followed. Unlike today's ATVs, these 1970s models all came with three tires.

> **MAN-TASTIC FACT**
>
> Can-Am has created a three-wheel motorcycle/car for driving fun, but the two wheels are in the front now for safety. This Can-Am Spyder was even featured in *Transformers 2* battling Decepticons.

Suzuki was the first to introduce the four-wheel (quads) ATV with their wildly successful QuadRacer line in 1982, but all of the companies soon followed suit. These four-wheelers are also significantly more powerful than the original 7-horsepower Honda US90. Today's quads are routinely sold with engines as big as most motorcycles on the road. After all, if you are going to shoot a rooster tail of dirt, you want it to go really high up.

Today, the Can-Am Renegade is the undisputed king of the quad heap. The bike stops on a dime and handles like a sophomore girl on prom night. It also looks just like a Transformer. I imagine at night this bright yellow machine unfolds to save the world from the evil Decepticons. And when it is not saving the world, it is letting men raise a little hell.

PICKUP TRUCKS

There is nothing like a pickup truck to tell the world, "I am strong. I am manly. And I have a place to carry my stuff." A truck tells the world that you are ready to do what needs to be done. Besides, if you have a truck, you will always have friends (who want you to help them move *their* stuff). At least when you move your guy friends, you will get paid in that precious man commodity: beer. And if you help your girlfriend move, you will probably get paid with a more precious man commodity. Yes, the pickup truck is a worthwhile manvention.

Men have always had the desire and the need to move lots of stuff, so pickups were a natural outgrowth of gasoline-powered engines. Many people consider the first pickup truck to be the International Harvester (IH) Auto Wagon, which was built in 1907. IH was a leading maker of farm machinery, and the Auto Wagon was a light-duty pickup built so farmers could haul their stuff. But these Auto Wagons were farm tools, not the popular transportation vehicles of today.

Some of the other early pickup trucks were homemade by modifying a car chassis or frame. Ever the business man, Henry Ford actually realized this early and catered to this market. He offered a Model TT chassis starting in 1917 that included a beefed-up suspension. This Model TT was most often sold

MAN-TASTIC FACT

Drivers in Thailand buy the second-greatest number of pickup trucks in the world. Trucks sell in Thailand because of the heavy tax on passenger cars.

MAN-DATE

In 1922, Henry Ford wrote in his autobiography: "Any customer can have a car painted any colour that he wants so long as it is black." But from 1908 to 1914, Model Ts were sold in a variety of colors. Black was eventually the only color because it was cheap and dried fast.

with just a cab so manly men could add their own wooden truck bed to the back, but the Model TT was soon to have a little competition.

The Dodge brothers built most of the Model T parts prior to starting their own company, and in 1914 they built their first car. It was bigger, more expensive, more powerful, and had more amenities than the Model T. Customers begged them for a truck, but it took the help of the U.S. government to start Dodge down the truck path. In 1917, the U.S. government contracted Dodge for 20,000 trucks for use in World War I. These trucks were used for ambulances, repair trucks, and cargo trucks. Dodge was chosen over Ford because Dodge's incredibly powerful 212-cubic-inch engine delivered a whopping 35 horsepower. Dodge eventually used this same chassis to start producing commercial delivery trucks after the war.

Pickup truck sales have exploded over the years, and now in the neighborhood of three million units a year are sold in the United States. Over the years, extended cab versions have appeared on the market to allow us to transport our entire

family but still maintain the manliness of a pickup. Now we can have families and avoid the curse of the minivan—something that gives us plenty of room but is not in any way a cool manvention. So all hail the only vehicle that says to the world: "I have shit and I know how to carry it."

BUMPER NUTS

In today's politically-correct-I-don't-want-to-offend-anybody world, we often have to bite our tongue. Most of the time, we seethe on the inside and wish we had the nuts to say what we felt in our heart. Well, if your set doesn't get enough use, you can always employ the not-so-subtle way to show the world you have a set. The all-purpose truck accessory that every man needs: a set of all-metal balls hanging from your trailer hitch.

Bumper nuts are over eight inches of anatomically correct metal balls that show the world what you are packing—or at least what is hanging from your trailer hitch. You can get them in any color at *www.bumpernuts.com.* Camo? No problem. Flesh colored? Gross, but still no problem. You can

MAN-TASTIC FACT

In the stagecoach days, a guard would sit in the right-hand seat of the stagecoach. This guard would often carry a shotgun and was said to be "riding shotgun." Hollering "Shotgun!" will get you the front seat next to the driver even today.

even buy blue balls as a gag for a friend getting married—or maybe one who has been married too long. A few companies even sell you a matching mini set for your keychain. But you might want to buy them now.

At least one state, Virginia, is already trying to outlaw the fake nut sacks hanging from many trucks. Looks like the morality police are at work here, but it doesn't make any sense. Fake nuts might be outlawed, but the shiny mud-flap girl is okay? Men need a way to express themselves, and in today's gender-neutral world, bumper nuts are the perfect manvention to say "I don't give a shit what you think."

MAN-DATE

It is illegal to pump your own gas in New Jersey. In 1949, the state decided that only trained professionals should be trusted to dispense flammable liquids into cars.

THE TOP TEN MANLIEST TV SHOWS EVER

1. *The Man Show*
2. *Deadliest Catch*
3. *Band of Brothers*
4. *MacGyver*
5. *South Park*
6. *SportsCenter*
7. *1000 Ways to Die*
8. *The A-Team*
9. *The Simpsons*
10. *Man vs. Wild*

INDEX

IMAGE CREDITS

Guitar © NeubauWelt
Car © NeubauWelt
Superhero © iStockphoto/4x6
Wrestlers © iStockphoto/4x6
Golf Cart © iStockphoto/fckuen
Men's Underwear © iStockphoto/studio524
Surfers © iStockphoto/4x6
Soccer © iStockphoto/vizualbyte
Cleat © iStockphoto/jfelton
Hockey © iStockphoto/XonkArts
BMX © NeubauWelt
Microwave © iStockphoto/imannaggia
Bottle opener © iStockphoto/SongSpeckels
Jack daniels © NeubauWelt
Grill © iStockphoto/ULTRA_GENERIC
Gas Grill/utensils © iStockphoto/diane555
Beer bottles © NeubauWelt
Paintball gun © iStockphoto/woewchikyury
Rollercoaster © iStockphoto/A-Digit
Jeans © iStockphoto/aunaauna
3D Glasses © iStockphoto/bubaone
Remote © iStockphoto/boroda003
Alarm clock © iStockphoto/cudazi
iPhone © iStockphoto/daboost
Rock Paper Scissors © iStockphoto/piart
Cards © iStockphoto/carol_woodcock
Fireworks © iStockphoto/MrPlumo
Swiss Army Knife © iStockphoto/A-Digit
Leafblower © iStockphoto/dondesigns
Chainsaw © iStockphoto/bubaone
Bikini © iStockphoto/LuciaCantone
Lawnmower © iStockphoto/mamado
Motorcycle © iStockphoto/paci77
Pickup Truck © iStockphoto/Somus

ABOUT THE AUTHOR

Bobby Mercer received his BA in Science Education from the University of Central Florida and his MA in Physics Education from the University of Virginia in 2008. He has twenty years' experience as a high school physics teacher and has won many teaching awards, including Teacher of the Year at Orlando Oak Ridge High School, Walt Disney's Teacherriffic Award, Who's Who in American Education, and the Outstanding Aerospace Educator Award. Bobby is the author of *Quarterback Dad* and *How Do You Light a Fart?* He lives in North Carolina with his wife, a family physician, and their daughters Nicole and Jordan.